Praise for *SMILE*

"A quick read that has the potential to transform your life! A practical and playful guide that skillfully teaches self-awareness. I highly recommend it for adults of all ages."

~ Mary Jo Kreitzer, PhD, RN, FAAN, Director, Center for Spirituality and Healing (CSH), University of Minnesota ~

~

"Simple, straightforward, easy-to-read, and fun! A unique and practical way to reduce stress and increase happiness, without stressing over it!"

~ Dennis J. Grubich, MSSW, LICSW, former Senior Mental Health Therapist, Wilder Foundation ~

~

"Saign's hard-earned insights into cultivating self-compassion, human decency and mercy is a much-needed message to us all."

~ Helen Wells O'Brien, M.Ed., M.Div., Board Certified Chaplain in a children's hospital ~

~

"Simple tools to change your brain and be more engaged in living!"

~ Cori M. Hildebrandt, MA LPC, Mediator, Meditator, and Psychotherapist ~

~

"A practical guide to find the positives in life, and strategies to make your rainy days have a bit more sunshine. A great reminder of how many things can be so simple, and beautiful."

~ Megan Ramirez, DO Obstetrician Gynecologist ~

~

"Saign's new book is designed to reframe your point of view and clear the mind for intentional decision-making and productive communication."

~ Ken Epstein, PhD, researcher and inventor with 35 years of experience working in corporate America ~

~

"Mr. Saign writes with a compassionate tone and empathic understanding of what it is like to be stricken by chronically anxious states. He beautifully paces education with pragmatic exercises which guides the reader in making anxiety an ally once again."

~ Joseph E. McEllistrem, Ph.D., Psychologist ~

~

"An inspiring and empowering journey to help us use intelligence in response to life's lovely chaos and challenges so that we can seize the day!"

~ Linda Gaveske, RN ~

~

"Geoffrey Saign's Smile More Stress Less will be my go-to guide for years to come and I will use it to support my clients, many of whom are concerned about the lows in life that are part of the everyday human experience."

~ Dr. Charlene Myklebust, Psy.D., named "Educator of the Year" by the National Alliance on Mental Illness—Minnesota, and a Hawn Foundation MindUp consultant ~

SMILE MORE MORE

STRESS LESS

· · · · · · · · · ● ● ● ● ● ● ● ● ● · · · · · · · ·

A Playful Method to End Anxiety,
Be Calm & Achieve Happiness
with Awareness

GEOFFREY SAIGN

Interior design by Lazar Kackarovski

Printed in the United States of America
ISBN: 979-8-698293-18-7 (ppbk)

Books by Geoffrey Saign

Nonfiction

Smile More Stress Less:
A Playful Guide to End Anxiety, Be Calm,
& Achieve Happiness with Awareness

Green Essentials: What You Need to
Know About the Environment

African Cats

Great Apes

Fiction

Jack Steel Action Mystery Thrillers

Steel Trust

Steel Force

Steel Assassin

Steel Justice

Alex Sight Action Mystery Thrillers

Kill Sight

Magical Beasts

Guardian: The Choice

Guardian: The Quest

Guardian: The Sacrifice

Guardian: The Stand

For Theresa...

Table of Contents

Introduction 1

Author's Note 3

PART 1: STRESS & LIFE

Chapter 1:   Defining HERE, Intelligence, Illusions, & Mind 5

Chapter 2:   The Most Important Thing in Life. 10

Chapter 3:   How Does Self-Created Stress Affect Our Lives? 18

PART 2: PLAYFUL EXAGGERATIONS

Chapter 4:   Interrupting Neural Pathways
             to End Self-Created Stress 28

Chapter 5:   Physical Techniques for Stress Reduction:
             Breathing, Body Scans, & More 41

Chapter 6:   Intuition & Self-Created Stress 45

Chapter 7:   Strong Self-Created Stress Reactions & Trauma 59

Chapter 8:   Goals & Visualization, Acceptance,
             & Expect the Unexpected 68

Chapter 9:   Labels, Contradictions, & HERE 83

Chapter 10: Letting Go of Conflict, Rumors, & Opinions 96

Chapter 11: Love, Kindness, & Loneliness 108

Chapter 12: Healthy Brain & Nature, Body Intelligence,
             & Real-World Stressful Problems 123

PART 3: POWER EXERCISES

Chapter 13: Drama-Free Living with Names & Pronouns
             (Power Exercises #1 & #2) 138

Chapter 14: Psychological Time & Location
             (Power Exercises #3 & #4) 159

Chapter 15: Mind Chatter 174

Chapter 16: Power Questions 179

Chapter 17: More Play for Persistent Rote Neural Patterns 182

Chapter 18: A Quick Summary 194

Author's Note 198

Bibliography 199

Acknowledgments 202

About the Author 203

Introduction

This book is the culmination of fifty years of arduous work. It's an easy, fun shortcut for you to reduce all stress in your life without going through all the struggles I endured to achieve success.

I was traumatized by a move at age seven. The intense fear and anxiety I experienced motivated me to look inward. I was also bullied in high school. In an attempt to end my fear, at age fifteen I was already practicing mindfulness.

Twenty-five years ago I began experiencing breakthroughs in mind-brain-body awareness, but I couldn't fit it all together and end my brain's stress-producing negative conditioning.

In 2018 my mind-brain-body awareness shifted significantly again, but I still didn't have a comprehensive understanding of how to fundamentally end stress, i.e., change my brain's thought process.

Then in 2020 a major breakthrough finally showed me a clear path to *Living with Intelligence HERE*.

Intelligence and HERE, as used in this book, will be defined in Chapter 1.

If you change your brain, you will change your world. Then you can change the whole world.

My life has never been the same. Neither will yours.

~

ABOUT THE AUTHOR

Geoffrey Saign began his inward journey by practicing mindfulness at the age of fifteen. For fifty years he studied many modalities for mind-body calming and awareness, including Qigong, tai chi, kung fu, meditation, biofeedback, positive psychology, and many others. He co-designed and taught a cutting-edge, research-based self-awareness class to young adults for ten years. In 2020 the author experienced a major breakthrough in mind-brain-body awareness, which led to *Living with Intelligence HERE*—and the resulting book, *Smile More Stress Less*.

He hopes this book will help readers of all ages reduce their own stress.

Author's Note

This book takes a different approach than most—if not all—books about stress. Thus, even if you know a lot about 'stress', it is strongly suggested that you read Chapters 1-3, which cover the basics but with a different slant.

This is a book about all of life. If you have conflict in any area of life, you have stress. Thus, to be free of stress, you have to be free of stress everywhere, in all areas.

○ **PART 1:** Chapters 1-3 look at the mechanics of stress and definitions used in this book. These chapters also prepare you for the mindset of this book, which is to learn to *Live with Intelligence HERE*, and PART 2.

○ **PART 2**: Chapters 4-12 introduce the **Playful Exaggerations** used to end stress in all areas of life. These chapters also prepare you for PART 3.

○ **PART 3:** Chapters 13-17 introduces **Power Exercises** that use Playful Exaggerations in powerful ways to end stress and rote neural patterns. We introduce **Power Questions** to allow the brain to make quantum leaps, and more Playful Exaggerations to end Mind Chatter.

PART 1
STRESS & LIFE

Defining HERE, Intelligence, Illusions, & Mind

If you know where you're headed,
it's easier to get there.

I t's important to understand the goal of this book. Knowing the endpoint will guide your brain, body, and mind's energy to always look in the direction we are aiming.

Goal: End all negative stress by learning how to live with Intelligence HERE.

To understand this goal, we need to define what we mean by HERE, Intelligence, Illusions, & Mind.

1) **HERE**

Definition: HERE is the immediate physical place where you are located, whether you are alone or with family, a partner, friends, or coworkers.

2) **Intelligence**

Definition: Intelligence is action in harmony with ourselves, others, and the planet HERE.

3) **Illusions**

Definition: Rote neural responses that create thoughts (words and images) that we accept as FACT.

4) **Mind**

Definition: Consciousness that has access to information and awareness beyond the physical brain, while coordinating with the brain and body for action. Mind operating without the barriers of fear, stress, anxiety, anger, disappointment, etc. results in intelligence. Mind connects us with everything and everyone with more information than thoughts can ever give us.

5) **Self-Created Stress**

Definition: Reacting negatively to ourselves, our thoughts, others, the environment, situations, or common occurrences in life. More simply, it is unnecessarily finding subjective fault with anything in life, and thus creating conflict and stress for yourself. It is also the primary way we create illusions. (Explained further in Chapter 2)

Now let's dive a little deeper into three of these definitions.

HERE

The definition for HERE is simple, right? HERE is wherever you are.

But *living* HERE is not so simple.

Example:

You are hiking in the woods. Instead of listening to the birds sing, you're obsessing about the person at work who said something rude to you. In effect, you are no longer fully aware HERE (in the woods), but are caught up in thoughts about a past** event. Or perhaps you're worrying about the traffic after the hike, caught up in thoughts about the future.**

In both cases, you are no longer fully aware HERE. Your attention is divided between your thoughts of the rude comment or traffic, and your surroundings. Your attention is divided between what you are sensing with your eyes and ears, and your inner thoughts and illusions. Being unaware can result in an accident if you trip and fall. If you are driving, you may total your car.

With divided attention, you also can't fully appreciate your surroundings or the people you are with.

Any time awareness or consciousness is divided, that IS stress.

The body operates HERE, as does the mind and intelligence. If you operate fully HERE, intelligence will lead you to the best path of action. Your job, therefore, is to live 100% HERE.

Intelligence

You may think, *Wait, people are intelligent! Isn't this supposed to be a book about lowering stress?*

I'm not talking about human intelligence to gain knowledge, make tools, etc., but about living in 100% harmony HERE, with clarity, awareness, and intelligence.

If people are intelligent, why do we stress ourselves in so many ways? Why are we so often in conflict with ourselves, each other, and the planet?

Without clarity, awareness, and intelligence, stress never ends. Living intelligently HERE is key to ending stress.

Intelligence is the brain, body, and mind working together in harmonious action, free of conflict, worry, fear, anxiety, annoyance, disappointment, etc. It is the joyful, creative expression of ourselves in action, and

always considers the best interests of ourselves, of others, and of the planet.

Living out of intelligence results in complete psychological security. Inner security maximizes your outer world security by living in a way that doesn't put yourself, others, or the planet into jeopardy.

Intelligence is timeless (i.e., not based on time). This means that intelligence always guides action HERE, and not in the future** or in the past**.

Intelligence is NOT living in *"the NOW"*" or in the *"present moment,"* but HERE.

If thought drives our action instead of intelligence, the results are obvious. Consider our planet, and the mess and chaos people have created as the direct result of *living out of thought and illusion instead of intelligence*. This has put all of us at risk for wars, permanent ecosystem damage, health issues from pollution, and food shortages.

Thought stems solely from the brain and offers a much more limited and conditioned response. Habits and addictions are two examples of slavishly following the brain's thought impulses.

Intelligence begins when we become aware of the brain's conditioned thought process, reject it, and change it.

Intelligence doesn't mean you ignore or refuse to seek out current information, or stop listening to your doctor, but it does mean you live out of peace, clarity, and harmony instead of stress and illusions.

Illusions

What prevents people from living intelligently HERE? What prevents us from having complete harmony in our lives?

The simple answer is illusions—created by our thought patterns.

The opposite of clarity, awareness, and intelligence is living and acting out of illusions.

Two areas the brain is constantly trying to organize for our security is action (what, when, how, and where we act) and our relationships with our family, friends, workmates, acquaintances, and strangers. However, instead of bringing us peace and security, this often creates stress, conflict, and illusions.

It's obvious that a schizophrenic who hears and talks to voices in their head is living in a world of illusions created by their brain's thought process.

Yet truthfully, almost all people live with nonstop, self-created illusions that make them miserable. And almost everyone is unaware they're living in a fantasy world of their own making.

The violence and chaos worldwide, along with the chronic negative emotions many of us carry, are proof that most of us are living out of illusions. Wars, conflicts, suppression of women, planet-wide environmental crises, racism, pollution, toxic chemicals that choke our health and our children's health, stress, sadness, depression, and dishonesty are all caused by NOT living with intelligence HERE. This is the direct result of allowing illusions to run our lives.

Experiencing unnecessary worry, stress, anxiety, disappointment, etc. means you are living out of illusions—the two go hand in hand. Even if you don't feel much stress, your thought process is still creating illusions nonstop.

1) **Illusions = stress.**

2) **Most of the thought process produces illusions.**

3) **True psychological freedom in life is ending the mindless reaction to your brain's rote neural responses that create these thoughts and illusions.**

So, what do we do?

CHAPTER 2

The Most Important Thing in Life

What are we all living for?

Love, Harmony, Awareness, and Enlightenment.

These words all point to a stress-free life, operating out of intelligence, full of love for ourselves and others in our relationships. This allows for inner peace and more smiles, joy, and happiness.

To have inner peace, we must end inner conflict (psychological stress) and outer conflict with others and our world. By not creating pain, you open yourself up to joy.

Is there a way to end all stress and conflict in most areas of our lives?

Yes!

~

HOW THE BRAIN CREATES STRESS

1) We observe something factual with our senses (sight, smell, hearing, touch, taste).

   Example:

   We see it is raining outside.

2) We react negatively to our factual observation. For example, we may say or think:

   Crap! Another lousy weather day!

3) We believe our negative reaction is a FACT and think or say:

   (I believe) It really is another lousy weather day!

4) We continue to create more negative thoughts or negative emotions.

   This rain sucks! What a horrible day!

   And/or we feel glum, disappointed, etc.

5) We speak, act, or continue thinking out of that negative emotional reaction:

   We tell others how much we hate rain, or that the weather is crappy, or thoughts along that line.

   The negative emotion affects us until the rain ends— and often much longer.

To end stress we have to change #2 through #5 on the list above. Specifically, #2—our negative reactions to what we observe with our senses.

What causes our underlying negative reactions to what we observe?

Different backgrounds or beliefs lead to different stress reactions. English speakers may have different words trigger stress than people who speak other languages. People of different ages may also react differently. People with different careers may have a different lens through which they view the world, which may cause different stress responses. A biologist may react more strongly to environmental issues, while an accountant may react more negatively to economic concerns.

Some words or phrases that may tell us we're reacting negatively to something in our lives are: *struggling with, tired of, I need, I hate, bored, exhausted, freaking, stressed, grumpy, sick of, fed up, hurting, numb, don't feel, begging, honestly, no clue, ugh, sucks, crappy, bleh, worse, miserable, icky,* or *I've lost it!* These words indicate negative reactions as in #2 above and can quickly trigger negative emotions.[1]

Emotions from past events can trigger thoughts in many directions. Sometimes the events are obvious to us—a near-death experience or traumatic accident. But sometimes they are more subtle.

There are many triggers that can lead to our negative reactions. Sometimes people spend years in therapy to discover their triggers, their hidden emotional past. But we can also look at the thought process and change our reactions to the triggers at the source—in our brain's neural programming.

Everyone, even with different negative reaction triggers, is operating from the same brain process. People with different languages, careers, ages, or other variables still end up with the same stress creation process. They react negatively to what they observe with their senses.

~

SO, WHAT CAN WE DO?

As Albert Einstein said, "*Insanity is doing the same thing over and over again and expecting different results,*" and "*No problem can be solved from the same level of consciousness that created it.*"

To truly end the stress process, we have to permanently change how our brain works. Otherwise we will repeat negative thoughts and emotions over and over until we die. We need to "wake up" and free the brain from incessant mind/thought chatter formed by old neural net patterns that we established in childhood and only added to as we matured.

The thought process is regarded as a sign of human intelligence, yet our thoughts often sabotage what we do and are unaware, negative, and create stress. We're running an old program in our brain's neural net. Worse, we're *addicted* to the repetitive thought process. It feels good, safe, right. It feels like *us*. *Who we are.* Our thoughts create feelings and emotions which, even if we don't always like them, are a known process that continually reinforces itself in the brain.

Minor adjustments are not enough to alter the brain's stress process. The brain's neural net needs a system overhaul, a complete update and reboot. We're going to take thought off its pedestal and get real with it.

Too often we feel that to attain awareness means taking a very serious, "adult" approach to life, like a monk sitting in a cave for a decade. But it can be a playful adventure with childlike wonder.

~

IS ALL STRESS BAD?

No. We need some stress, or we'll vegetate in a chair and do nothing. Physical stress from your body motivates you to empty your bladder, eat, or drink water. Babies cry when hungry. You need financial motivation to get a job. You need to run to the bus stop so you don't miss the bus. You need some stress to accomplish goals.

~

WHAT IS SELF-CREATED STRESS?

As stated earlier: *Self-Created Stress* **is defined in this book as reacting negatively to ourselves, our thoughts, others, the environment, situations, or common occurrences in life. More simply, it is unnecessarily finding subjective fault with anything in life, and thus creating conflict and stress for yourself. It is also the primary way we create illusions.**

Self-Created Stress is directly related to our emotional reactions to our thoughts. The entire human race runs by their thought patterns. To be truly free of stress, we have to be free of negative reactions to the thought patterns in our neural net, i.e., in our brain. We have to change our brain's neural pathways.

Stating facts is not a negative reaction. For example, if you say, *That table is inexpensive because it uses cheap materials*, it's not a negative reaction, but a fact. Thinking or saying, *I hate eating on cheap furniture!* or *What a piece of crap!* are negative reactions.

For each of us, different words in our thoughts can create different levels of stress. Our language and how we talk to ourselves matters. As we become more aware of how our thought patterns affect us, it is easier to change the words we use to talk to ourselves.

If you find yourself saying things such as, *He stressed me out!* or *That situation stressed me out!* remember this:

You create your stress by how you react to people, situations, or events. Blaming your parents, past relationships, your job, the economy, politicians, the weather, etc. for your worries, fear, stress, disappointments, anger, etc.

won't end these negative emotions, because you create them.

Obviously some people and situations are much more challenging to handle than others. Sometimes we can remove those situations or people from our lives, and sometimes we cannot.

But we can always change how we respond to difficult situations, people, and life's challenges.

The good news is: **If you accept responsibility for creating your stress, then you can take action by changing your neural patterns.** You will be able to end the Self-Created Stress that has enslaved you.

*Why does it matter if we have negative reactions
to our world, people, or ourselves?*

Negative reactions create conflict, unpleasant feelings, and lock us into needing certain things to feel at peace. We become servants to our negative reactions and our thought patterns, *Servants* to our patterned brains instead of *Masters* of them. Most of our brain patterns were set up when we were unaware and not masters of our brains. Time to take back control.

Research suggests that thought travels along some neurons as fast as 70-120 m/s (miles per second) or 156-270 mph (miles per hour).[2] We don't have the technology to measure the exact speed of thought, but your thoughts pass through your brain faster than you blink your eye. You may not even know what thoughts in the background are making you react the way you do.

*Negative Stress affects everyone.
The United States is one of the most stressed-out
countries in the world.*

I live in Minnesota. People here often complain about the weather. *The snow is a nightmare, I'll never get to work! The rain will never stop. It's too cold out to survive! It's hot enough to fry an egg on the pavement. It's unbelievably humid, muggy, stifling, a killer!*

Why does it matter if you react negatively to a weather pattern, such as a rainy day? There are many rainy days, cold days, humid days, and windy days over a lifetime. If a weather pattern triggers a negative reaction in you, the result is the same. Conflict. Unhappiness. Worry.

There are a million things that can upset us if we react negatively to them. A million ways to be bothered by a situation, person, or what we are sensing. A million ways to find fault with ourselves, nature, or anything else in the world.

These negative reactions are all a form of stress, often based on an underlying concern that something will take away our happiness, block our goals, or not live up to our expectations. All of these reactions limit and reduce our moments for happiness and joy.

You might be unhappy or in conflict when you experience:

○ *Horrible traffic.*

○ *Can't find my keys.*

○ *The coffee maker broke.*

○ *My co-workers always complain about the boss.*

○ *My family members/friends don't listen to me.*

○ *Politicians vote against my interests.*

○ *The movie was lousy.*

○ *My partner left me.*

○ *I failed at a goal.*

○ *I didn't get a raise.*

○ *A flat tire. A broken computer. A stubbed toe. A snippet of gossip.*

It's an endless list.

It doesn't matter if you react with anxiety, fear, impatience, disappointment, anger, or other painful emotions, the result is the same: conflict with what is happening. You are rejecting the particular HERE you are experiencing. You are in effect saying, *I don't want this!* or *This isn't good enough!*

When you reject HERE, the situation and place where you are right now, you are rejecting the only HERE that you have. No future is promised or guaranteed for any of us, so we better enjoy what we have HERE.

If you reject HERE, for any reason, you are in conflict with your world at that moment.

You have created conflict, unhappiness, and discontent inside yourself.

Self-Created Stress applies to anything in life you decide isn't what you want to experience HERE, even though you are.

It's that simple. And that complex.

This doesn't mean you should accept situations and never change. But it does mean that negative reactions to any situation affects your level of inner peace, joy, and happiness.

If you're not aware of the thoughts causing your stress, how can you change them?

Simple. By doing the easy, playful exercises in this book, you slow down the reaction process of your brain and become more self-aware, more conscious of all your thoughts. If you take control of your thought process, you will leave stress, worry, anxiety, anger, disappointment, and fear behind. It will allow you to be peaceful and calm at the same time. This is something anyone can achieve at any age.

CHAPTER 3

How Does Self-Created Stress Affect Our Lives?

*Stress is an equal opportunity problem
that affects everyone.*

I f we're going to invest in fundamentally changing the brain, it's important to understand why the human brain has led us to stressful interactions.

Stress happens if you are rich or poor, a high school dropout or a PhD, young or old, whatever your demographic. Why?

OUR BRAINS ARE HARDWIRED TO LOOK FOR THREATS AND DANGER

People have been worried and stressed for thousands of years.

How and why did such patterns develop in the human brain?

Our brains are hardwired to look for, and pay attention to, threats or danger. It was a survival mechanism. *I must remember that the saber-toothed tiger lives over the hill, because he will eat me if I cross into his territory.* Focusing, even obsessing, on the saber-toothed tiger was necessary for survival. This was also true for storms and other elemental events. Without an obsessive focus on survival, saber-toothed tigers would have eaten many more people.

When two neurons (brain cells) respond to a stimulus (such as a spoken word or thought), they form chemical and physical pathways to each other, which are strengthened or weakened depending on how often they are co-activated. This process of "neurons that fire together, wire together" is the basis for all learning.[3]

Neural connections related to life or death situations become even stronger, especially if an emotion such as fear or anger is attached to the thought. This is also true if a strong positive emotion such as joy is attached to the thought.

Repeating a particular thought over and over with a strong negative emotion, such as fear, strengthens the neural connections associated with that thought and memory, making it easier for the brain to recall it and repeat it. Every time a person went out of the cave and saw a particular hill, their brain would default to, *The saber-toothed tiger lives over that hill, be careful!*

> **Thought + strong emotion (fear, worry, anxiety, joy, happiness etc.) = Stronger neural connections in the brain.**

It's as if the brain gets grooved like a vinyl record. The strongest and deepest grooves are the first ones the brain searches for and "plays" when we encounter similar situations, problems, people, or challenges.

Example:

Let's say that every time we see *a rainy day*, or *Fred*— someone we don't like, we respond the same way— e.g., *Rain sucks!* or *I can't stand Fred!*

The brain reacts mechanically, without any conscious input or awareness, by accessing the "grooved" track of strong neural net connections. Worse, we believe this mechanical negative reaction is a FACT. We believe *Rain sucks!* or that *Fred is someone I cannot tolerate!* Let's assume Fred isn't a maniac, but just annoying.

Eventually the **brain is running us** instead of **us running our brain**. We're no longer masters of our action and brain, but slavishly reacting over and over again with patterns we've wired into our own brain. This zombie-like, unaware existence creates conflict with others, with our world, and within ourselves.

In today's modern world we still need the ability to react strongly to threats. We must be able to assess risks, though our current saber-toothed tigers may be reckless drivers and/or other potentially dangerous situations. There is obvious survival value in recognizing situations such as, *Don't walk out into traffic!* or *Don't put your hand in the fire!*

However, the modern mind and brain seem to have expanded this ancient survival response to create tigers that don't exist. This repetition increases and maintains unnecessary Self-Created Stress in our lives.

It's as if the brain is trying to protect itself from all things that *we don't like or find irritating.* The brain has equated *don't like* and *find irritating* as a threat to our survival.

Is dislike or irritation something we want to reinforce over and over as *bad* or *horrible*, and react every time we encounter it?

A rainy day or criticism is **not** a survival issue. Completing simple tasks is **not** a survival issue. Seeing Fred is **not** a survival issue.

Repeating negative reactions to things you don't like or want to avoid creates a negative reaction cycle that leads to conflict inside of us.

Conflict is not harmony, peace, or happiness.

It is also not aware.

Being unaware allows for missed opportunities.

○ *Opportunities to be happy.*

○ *To feel love. To give love.*

○ *To learn. To help others learn.*

○ *To discover something new.*

○ *To be creative.*

○ *To see beauty.*

○ *To be surprised.*

○ *To have fun!*

Life is too short to miss any opportunities to smile, say something positive, or be happy and feel loved. Every situation is precious.

THE GOOD NEWS IS, YOU CAN END SELF-CREATED STRESS!

Current research shows that the brain is capable of change at any age. Neuroscientists call it brain plasticity; the extraordinary ability of the brain to create new neural pathways, or alter existing ones, in response to new experiences or information.[4]

You can permanently change your brain's negative stress responses and neural wiring! You can become the master of your brain instead of a servant to old, habitual neural pathways created when you were younger and didn't understand what you were doing.

The brain is simply doing what evolution (and our current consciousness) taught it, so it could survive threats and danger, either real or perceived. You are going to re-teach the brain how to *live with intelligence HERE.*

Even if we have very strong, repeated reactions that we have reinforced for years or decades in the brain, we can change these patterns, FAST. You created the negative stress reaction, and you can end it.

Just like building muscle, helping your brain change requires daily exercise. You can weaken the repetitive, mechanical reactions (old neural programming), and strengthen positive neural patterns, allowing more peace, spontaneity, joy, happiness, and playfulness into your life.

Before we begin these exercises, it's important to understand and become aware of how Self-Created Stress can affect our lives.

HOW SELF-CREATED STRESS AFFECTS OUR LIVES

Unfortunately, Self-Created Stress is more than just a habit of reacting negatively to things. It affects us much more deeply than that.

1) Self-Created Stress creates a world of worry, insecurity, and disappointment, and the belief that life should *be and happen the way we want and expect it to.* This makes us inflexible, repeatedly reacting to situations the same way—like robots.

2) Self-Created Stress perpetuates the myth that we can easily lose our inner peace and happiness. It makes inner peace and happiness feel fragile and unstable.

3) Self-Created Stress blocks intuition, our natural intelligence that guides us along our way.

4) Self-Created Stress is the number one underlying cause of health problems[5] and one of the significant factors that can lead to dementia.[6]

5) Self-Created Stress limits our ability to be loving or kind. It separates and isolates us from people and nature HERE, weakening all our relationships.

6) Self-Created Stress creates the illusion that everything is *"the same,"* e.g., that all *"rainy days"* are the same, when they are not. Every situation is unique. Every HERE is unique. But habitual reactions create the illusion of *sameness* and the resultant negativity or boredom.

7) Self-Created Stress focuses our energy on negative thinking.

8) Self-Created Stress blinds us to beauty.

9) Self-Created Stress creates conflict with others, the world around us, and ourselves.

10) Self-Created Stress makes us critical of ourselves and others.

11) Self-Created Stress negatively affects anyone who listens to our reactive negative viewpoints and reactions. Children learn by watching adults. Most children's brain patterns are set by age five,[7] so it's critical for the adults in their lives to show awareness and flexibility, and teach them how to be free of rote stressful reactions to life (rote = mechanical, habitual, and without awareness).

12) Self-Created Stress is a habit that keeps us stuck in our lives. If you respond the same way to events or people every time you encounter them, you can't see anything new, nor can you respond with the aliveness and energy necessary to interact positively. You become a servant to the brain patterns you have repeated and reinforced, no longer a master of your brain and your life.

~

SELF-CREATED STRESS QUIZ

Take this simple 15-question quiz to find out how strongly Self-Created Stress operates in your own life.

(Give your answer for each question)

Where 0 = Never

        1 = Several times a year

        2 = Several times a month

        3 = Several times a week

        4 = Almost daily

1) How often do you complain about the weather?

0 (Never)   1   2   3   4 (almost daily)

2) How often are you annoyed or irritated by people? (family, students, friends, coworkers, or strangers)

0 (Never)   1   2   3   4 (almost daily)

3) How often are you worried, displeased, upset, or irritated by what happens at work or school?

0 (Never)   1   2   3   4 (almost daily)

4) How often are you disappointed or upset by world events or news?

0 (Never)   1   2   3   4 (almost daily)

5) How often do you spread Self-Created Stress to others with your words or actions in the form of complaints, criticisms, or gossip?

0 (Never)   1   2   3   4 (almost daily)

6) How often are you irritated while driving or using public transportation?

0 (Never)   1   2   3   4 (almost daily)

7) How often do you react with fear, worry, or anger to politics?

0 (Never)   *1*   *2*   *3*   *4 (almost daily)*

8) How often do you criticize or find fault with family, friends, students, coworkers, or strangers?

0 (Never)   *1*   *2*   *3*   *4 (almost daily)*

9) How often do you criticize or find fault with yourself?

0 (Never)   *1*   *2*   *3*   *4 (almost daily)*

10) How often do you react with worry, impatience, or anger to daily events (small or large) outside of work or school?

0 (Never)   *1*   *2*   *3*   *4 (almost daily)*

11) How often do you dwell on arguments, grudges, or complaints for days, weeks, months, or even years about someone or a situation that upset you?

0 (Never)   *1*   *2*   *3*   *4 (almost daily)*

12) How often do you find yourself tightening your stomach, fists, shoulders, jaw, or pursing your lips?

0 (Never)   *1*   *2*   *3*   *4 (almost daily)*

13) How often do you feel anxious, worried, upset, angry, panicked, impatient, disappointed, unhappy, lonely, or fearful?

0 (Never)   *1*   *2*   *3*   *4 (almost daily)*

14) How often do your thoughts obsessively go over the same situation, problem, challenge, or issue?

0 (Never)   *1*   *2*   *3*   *4 (almost daily)*

15) How often do you find yourself frowning?

0 (Never)   *1*   *2*   *3*   *4 (almost daily)*

SCORE YOUR QUIZ

Add up your points from the 15 questions and score yourself below.

- ○ If your answers were no higher than 1s, and you scored 0-15, you are largely free of Self-Created Stress, and are happy, joyful, and supportive of others and yourself. You find the good and positive in almost every situation. You have an easy time smiling. If you scored a 3 or 4 on any of the questions, there are some situations in your life that you still consistently react to with significant stress.

- ○ If your answers were no higher than 2s, and you scored 16-30, you are generally happy, but sometimes get caught up in Self-Created Stress and have moments where you focus on the negatives in life. It damps down your smile in some situations. If you scored a 3 or 4 on any of the questions, there are some situations in your life that you still consistently react to with significant stress.

- ○ If your answers were no higher than 3s, and you scored 31-45, you often get caught up in Self-Created Stress; life often feels hard, stressful, worrisome, difficult, and unpleasant. You would like to escape some of your current situations if you could. You often find yourself frowning, if not outwardly, then inwardly.

- ○ And if some or all of your answers were 4s, you scored 46-60, you're not happy or fulfilled in most areas of your life.

Whatever your score, don't worry! Self-Created Stress is a learned habit that you can easily unlearn. To change anything about yourself, it's important to understand what you wish to leave behind. Seeing how Self-Created Stress operates in your life is the first step to becoming free of it. You can and will become a new person!

Now let's get to it.

PART 2
PLAYFUL EXAGGERATIONS

CHAPTER 4

Interrupting Neural Pathways to End Self-Created Stress

*Remaining **calm** and **peaceful** inside and out
is one of our main goals.*

I f we remain calm, inner peace and joy are possible. Remaining calm inside and out should be your *primary goal*. No matter who you are, or where you are on your journey, you can be stress-free. Remaining calm maximizes your chances for good health and more smiles. Smiles are contagious and have the ability to instantly put us into a meditative state.[8] They joyfully bring your full attention to HERE.

The good news is that you don't have to chase being calm or happy. If you end Self-Created Stress, then calm, inner peace, and happiness will appear. Eliminate the negative, and the positive will be yours.

~

YOU CAN END DAILY STRESS WITH PLAYFULNESS AND HUMOR

As stated in Chapter 2, Self-Created Stress is a process that begins with the senses, followed by a negative reaction of thought. Let's look at another simple example.

Your partner (or child or roommate) didn't wash, rinse, and put away their dirty dishes, or did something else that annoys you. You think, *That idiot!* or other choice words.

Perhaps you also think, *Now I have to do the dishes! They never do their work! I'm sick of it!*

You decide to scold them, and maybe even play out an argument in your head in which you "yell" at them for minutes or even hours. You are lost in the illusions of this internal argument. You're not arguing with anyone in the room, just your own thoughts.

All the upset energy you create before you talk to the person is wasted while you are unhappy or irritated.

Later you mention the dirty dishes to the person with an edge to your voice, increasing the likelihood of a negative response from them.

Maybe you learn that the person had a valid reason for not doing the dishes; an emergency came up, or they became sick. All your energy building up to the negative interaction was wasted.

Even if the person doesn't have a valid or logical reason for leaving the dirty dishes, you still want to be able to control your stress.

Is it possible to see the dirty dishes and note them without reacting with Self-Created Stress? You can still tell your partner or child that they need to wash, rinse, and put away their dishes without upsetting yourself with negative emotions.

When you find yourself reacting with Self-Created Stress, take a moment and listen to the thoughts running through your mind and simply observe them, like fish in

an aquarium, without trying to add anything to them. This is one way to change your thought patterns and achieve calm.

You might still obsess over a situation you don't like, but if you practice this, the whole process of reacting negatively to anything will begin to fade away. All you have to do is pay attention.

You may still have to speak to the person/child about the dishes, or find a new roommate, or find a different solution, but you can do that calmly too, without stress, worry, or conflict.

~

Every time we change our thought pattern or interrupt old thought responses, we are changing our brain—teaching it—and allowing a new neural pattern to develop. We are telling the brain, *This old pattern of thought is no longer useful or acceptable.* The brain always listens. *EVERY SINGLE EFFORT IS WORTHWHILE.* This cannot be overstated.

~

Our INTENT in this process is the WHY of what we're doing. Our intent is to consciously break up our habitual neural pattern—mechanical, negative thoughts—by informing and teaching the brain to change. In essence, to rewire itself. If the brain understands what we are trying to do, and why, it will listen. It has no choice. You can be the master of wiring your neural net to a positive state. Research shows that even our DNA is flexible and changeable. Stress can cause adverse DNA changes, while positivity can change DNA for the better.[9]

So how do we actually do this?

MIND VS. BRAIN

We will use the mind to reflect back to the brain what it is doing. For simplicity, we'll refer to *Mind* as awareness/intelligence, and *Brain* as the physical structure in our skulls. Thought is patterned in the brain, and we need to change our pattern through awareness. Rote thought patterns make the brain rigid and inflexible when responding. Awareness can end habitual negative patterns and allow the brain's responses to be fluid, spontaneous, and creative, increasing awareness, calm, and joy.

Now let's practice!

~

Note: Do every exercise on the following **TRY THIS** and **PRACTICE** sections at least once. Practice strengthens understanding and leads to mastery.

At times you may think, *This exercise is silly and childish!* I assure you, these exercises work. They are *childlike*, not *childish*, which is a good thing. Children learn by being inquisitive and playful. Too often, adults lose this sense of playfulness in life and get stuck in ruts. So embrace your inner child in the following exercises!

We are trying to change a complicated process. This method produces serious and important results, and will allow changes at all levels in your brain and life.

TRY THIS

1)   One way to change rote, stressful thought patterns is to use playful exaggeration. It is a simple, repetitive method that will produce immediate and significant results, and we will use it often in this book in different ways and situations.

Let's try it with the dirty dishes. You see the dirty dishes in the sink. Thoughts enter your mind about how irresponsible the person was in leaving them there. You feel annoyed and irritated. You notice this Self-Created Stress reaction inside yourself, and you **interrupt** it. You say out loud or think:

Oh no! My hands will never recover from this!
This is going to ruin my whole life!
It's the end of the world as I know it!

Smile as you do this. Smiling brings about a strong positive emotion, and strong emotion helps change the brain by wiring a new neural pattern that's even stronger.

It's worth repeating that your brain pays attention to everything you focus on. If your intent is to end illusions, the brain will work on it, even if you don't see an immediate change in how you respond to situations with illusions.

- Be creative in your playful exaggerations. There is no right or wrong way to do this.

- Also be melodramatic, which is what a Self-Created Stress reaction is anyway. Be silly with your voice.

- Change your pitch and tone deep or high.

All of this forces you to put the dirty dishes problem (which is tiny) into proper context in the scheme of life. Playful exaggeration also allows you to remain calm and smile.

What if you get caught up in a rote reaction
and emotionally react?

No worries! Later, when free of the reaction, repeat the playful exaggerations. It helps prepare you for the next time you react negatively. Soon you will be interrupting your reactions as they occur.

Lastly, you are depersonalizing your habitual reactions, which may feel so strong and important that even now you might want to argue that *my opinions are important!*

Remember, the goals are to become aware of your stress patterns, interrupt them, become objective in

viewing them, and end them. These and other exercises in this book will help you do all of this naturally.

EXPECTED RESULTS

By interrupting your Self-Created Stress with playful exaggerations:

1) You increase your awareness of your rote responses by interrupting them.

2) You train your mind/self to not respond with negative emotions to your old Self-Created Stress patterns.

3) You effectively tell your brain you're not going to pay attention to the old neural patterns and want to end these rote responses and create new ones. (Intent)

At first you are consciously interrupting and ending the rote thought patterns. As you continue, the brain decreases the regurgitation of Self-Created Stress statements. Lastly, the brain rewires itself and begins to end Self-Created Stress thoughts on its own, because that is your INTENT for it. And the brain has no choice, it always listens! It is, after all, *your* brain.

Remember: Intelligence begins when we become aware of the brain's conditioned thought process, reject it, and change it.

Playful exaggeration can be a fun exercise to practice with any negative reaction. It can quickly end Self-Created Stress. In time, you won't need playful exaggerations, since you won't react with Self-Created Stress to small daily events.

Here are three more examples of using playful exaggeration to interrupt and reduce Self-Created Stress:

A) Let's say you spend a lot of time at school or work setting up a special event or meeting. After the event, another student or coworker says to you: *Someone else did it even better last year.* You react with Self-Created Stress and think, *How can they say that to me?!*

You notice the reaction, interrupt it, and exaggerate it:

I can't believe s/he said that to ME,
the World President!
or
It's worse than being dragged by elephants through
a pile of manure!

B)   You see a mouse, spider, or bee in the house. You shriek or react with dismay, worry, or distaste. You notice the reaction, interrupt it, and exaggerate it:

Oh no! It's an alien invasion to take over the world!
or
I'm living in a horror movie!

C)   Someone cuts in front of you on the freeway and didn't even use their blinker. You react with Self-Created Stress, impatience, or anger, and feel the impulse to honk your horn for several seconds or something worse. You notice this reaction, interrupt it, and playfully exaggerate it out loud or in your head:

I am Godzilla and they insulted me!
or
I will call in the great wizard and dissolve their car
into a pile of dust!

Smile while doing this!

○ One playful exaggeration is enough, but more than one is fine.

○ You can use the exaggerations supplied in this book, or be creative and change them randomly.

○ There is no need to memorize the playful exaggerations provided or *"do them perfectly."* What matters most is that you *interrupt* and contradict your Self-Created Stress neural patterns.

○ Even after the fact, or later when you are calmer, practicing playful exaggerations *will change your brain.*

○ When you think or say these playful exaggerations, try to visualize quick images of the elephant dragging you through manure, a wizard dissolving the car, an alien invasion, or yourself as Godzilla driving the car.

Imagination is good for the brain. It weakens the mechanical responses you are trying to stop.

Everyone has different abilities when it comes to visualizing images. If this is difficult for you, don't worry! Do what is easy for you, don't stress, and that's good enough. Your results won't be any less effective than a world class visualization expert.

Don't be critical of yourself in this process. Catch whatever Self-Created Stress statements you can, and don't worry about those you miss or get caught up in. Interrupt them when you can and continue. You'll automatically get better at this process as it becomes easier, more enjoyable, and more effective.

Never criticize yourself for not being imaginative enough, not being able to visualize, being too slow to learn, etc. I have been a turtle in many of my endeavors, but I've always crossed the finish line!

Another option for images is to think of TV shows, cable programs, cartoons, movies, songs, characters, storylines, and scenes. Humor helps, so make the exaggerations funny. Humor is wonderful for brain health, physical health, and reducing stress.

Example:

If someone cuts you off in rush hour traffic, interrupt your negative reaction and say, *How dare they cut off Superman when he's driving!* or *Bugs Bunny is not a happy camper!*

These are two well-known fictional characters, but there are thousands that you can use. Don't forget to smile.

Remember, you are trying to change neural patterns that have often been decades in the making. Be patient and kind to yourself as you begin this process. You are teaching your brain a new way to respond to situations, people, and events. The brain rarely change its responses immediately.

Whatever the situation, you can make it melodramatic, silly, or humorous. Put it in perspective to calm yourself, smile, and perhaps even chuckle, giggle, or laugh out loud.

PAUSE HERE TO CREATE THREE EXAMPLES OF PLAYFUL EXAGGERATION FOR RECENT SITUATIONS THAT YOU REACTED TO WITH SELF-CREATED STRESS.

A) Self-Created Stress Situation:

_____

B) Playful Exaggeration:

_____

Say, think, & visualize the playful exaggeration, and smile!

A) Self-Created Stress Situation:

_____

B) Playful Exaggeration:

_____

Say, think, & visualize the playful exaggeration, and smile!

A) Self-Created Stress Situation:

_____

B) Playful Exaggeration:

_____

Say, think, & visualize the playful exaggeration, and smile!

PRACTICE

A) Sit down with paper and pen (or a computer) and create a list of things that aggravate or frustrate you at family gatherings, at work, outdoors, with people, etc. Make the list as complete as possible.

B) Next write down playful exaggerations about each event.

C) Lastly say out loud or think the playful exaggeration in your head. Visualize images of your playful exaggerations and smile, even if it's forced.

This practice will make it easier for you to interrupt your reactions *as they occur*.

Example:

A) Frustrating situation:

It makes me upset when my friends always show up late for dinner.

B) Your playful exaggeration could be:

I'll have to eat my shoes to stay alive!

C) Say, think, & visualize the playful exaggeration, and smile!

PAUSE HERE TO WRITE DOWN THREE SITUATIONS FROM YOUR LIST THAT YOU OFTEN RESPOND TO WITH FRUSTRATION AND REPLACE THEM WITH PLAYFUL EXAGGERATIONS.

A) Frustrating Situation:

_____

B) Playful Exaggeration:

_____

Say, think, & visualize the playful exaggeration, and smile!

A) Frustrating Situation:

_____

B) Playful Exaggeration:

_____

Say, think, & visualize the playful exaggeration, and smile!

A) Frustrating Situation:

_____

B) Playful Exaggeration:

_____

Say, think, & visualize the playful exaggeration, and smile!

The next time you find yourself in one of these situations, try to interrupt your Self-Created Stress thoughts with a playful exaggeration. Don't give in to the old neural patterns!

A) Write down any negative feelings or emotions you have, past or current, about any area of your life. Maybe you wanted to go on to college basketball and didn't make the tryouts. Or a failed relationship still makes you sad.

B) Write down a playful exaggeration about the emotion or event.

C) Say, think, & visualize the playful exaggeration, and smile!

~

Note: The goal isn't to pretend events didn't happen, or to make light of them, but to end your rote stress reactions to them! It's therapeutic to end the repetitive stressful statements you tell yourself about your life's events. It's healthy to end the neural patterns in the brain that keep inflicting pain on yourself with negative reactions and emotions.

Example:

A) Negative emotion: *I still feel sad about breaking up with my girlfriend/boyfriend six months ago.*

B) Playful Exaggeration: *On a planet of 7.8 billion people, it's impossible to meet anyone else!*

A) Negative Emotion:

_____

B) Playful Exaggeration:

_____

Say, think, & visualize the playful exaggeration, and smile!

A) Negative Emotion:

_____

B) Playful Exaggeration:

_____

Say, think, & visualize the playful exaggeration, and smile!

A)   Negative Emotion:

_____

B)   Playful Exaggeration:

_____

Say, think, & visualize the playful exaggeration, and smile!

~

You don't need to meditate in a cave or follow a guru for awareness. Nobody knows your thoughts or your neural pattern intricacies better than you; everyone else only has secondhand information about your brain.

This doesn't mean you shouldn't talk to others about your problems, issues, or stress. It's helpful, good for support, and can give you insights into yourself. But getting into your brain and changing your neural patterns is up to you. By following these simple suggestions, you can succeed!

CHAPTER 5

Physical Techniques for Stress Reduction: Breathing, Body Scans, & More

Lifelong Techniques for Stress Reduction

B esides playful exaggerations, there are other techniques you can use for short-term stress reduction.

BREATHING

Deep breathing should be a constant in your life in all situations, especially when under stress.

During a negative Self-Created Stress reaction, pay attention to your breathing. Notice if you are taking short, quick, upper chest breaths, or holding your breath. Notice if you are tightening your chest, shoulders, jaw, or stomach. Relax your body by focusing on and relaxing the muscles you are tensing.

Now sit, stand, or lie on your back. Relax your body—see BODY SCAN below. Breathe in deeply by inhaling through the nose and gently pushing out the stomach. Breathe into your stomach first, then up through your torso and chest. Hold your breath for 2-4 seconds, then exhale slower than you inhaled— exhale through the mouth in reverse from your chest down to your stomach, pulling it in gently. This should be a relaxed breath without straining. Place attention on the air going in through your nostrils and out through your mouth.

Variations on the above deep breathing exercise have been used for over 5,000 years in Qigong, yoga, and meditation to calm the brain and nervous system, build energy, and improve health. Current research verifies this, and deep breathing is often referred to in western cultures as diaphragmatic breathing.

PAUSE HERE AND PRACTICE SIX BREATHS NOW.

(Close your eyes if you're not driving or doing some other activity that requires vision.)

~

BODY SCAN

Even if you are not aware of Self-Created Stress, your body will signal you.

When you are stressed, your heart might race, your stomach tightens, your shoulders bunch, your skin turns sweaty, or your jaw clenches. Perhaps you bite your nails or tap your feet. These are some of the visible signals that you are creating stress.

Stress reactions cause health problems. It's important to pay attention to the outward signs to know when we're inwardly creating stress.

How to do a Body Scan:

A) Sit or lie down and close your eyes (unless you're driving).

B) Take a very deep breath and exhale slowly. Then breathe normally (deep breathing without straining).

C) Beginning with your feet, pay attention to any foot muscle tension, and relax those muscles. Next move up to your calves and do the same thing.

D) Repeat this process with your upper legs, butt, hips, hands, arms, back, stomach, chest, shoulders, neck, jaw, and face. Pause in each area a few moments to see if you notice tension. If so, relax those muscles. This is a body scan.

Take one minute to do a body scan every night in your bed just before going to sleep. It will help you fall asleep. Or do a body scan while sitting or standing in a line. In time you will become very aware of tension in any muscle in your body when Self-Created Stress occurs, and easily release it in seconds.

Everyone holds tension in different places. Learn your own patterns and they will quickly disappear.

Relaxing the body will relax your mind and thoughts and allow you to become more aware of the underlying thought patterns causing stress.

PAUSE HERE AND TAKE A MINUTE TO DO A FULL BODY SCAN NOW.

~

EXTENDED BODY SCAN FOR SLEEP

You can extend the body scan with the following messages to your body just before going to sleep. Focus on each area briefly as you name it.

"When my head hits the pillow, my whole body and being will relax. My feet, legs, hands, arms, hips, back, stomach muscles, chest, jaw, neck, face, and scalp will relax. My skin will relax. My heart, kidneys, lungs, stomach, intestines, liver, lungs, spleen, and kidneys

will relax. My brain and my thoughts will relax. My glands will all relax. My blood running through all my veins and arteries will relax. My cells will relax. My energy will relax. My whole being will settle into a very deep, restful, and healing sleep. I will wake up refreshed, alert, and smiling."

Often you will fall asleep before you finish this. There is no perfect or right or wrong way to do this, so there's no need to memorize it. Do what feels right for you.

~

MORE PHYSICAL SUGGESTIONS FOR STRESS REDUCTION

1) Remove yourself from the situation: e.g., if you are at work, get up and walk away from your desk.

2) Exercise: Go for a walk, swim, bike, or perform a physical activity you enjoy. Physical exercise takes us out of our heads and into our bodies, relieving mental stress. Research shows that spending time in nature is one of the healthiest things you can do for your brain and mind.

3) Smile. Even if you don't want to, don't feel happy, or have no reason to smile, force it. Forced smiling, like forced laughter, results in many of the same benefits that natural smiles provide. Smiling forces the thought process to slow down or stop. It's one of the reasons we feel good when we smile naturally. You are instantly in a meditative happy place HERE. So when you are anxious, stressed, or worried—smile!

Smiling also helps us learn to not take our thoughts and ourselves so seriously. If we often think everything is a do-or-die event, smiling helps put things into a healthier perspective.

CHAPTER 6

Intuition & Self-Created Stress

Trust yourself more than anyone else.

I ntuition is the beginning whispers of intelligence **HERE.** It doesn't mean we are living free of illusions; rather, intuition is intelligence cutting through the illusions for brief glimpses of the best course of action HERE. Thus it's worthwhile taking a look at how intuition operates in our lives, and how Self-Created Stress short-circuits it. Intuition can help if you suffer from anxiety and stress when you make decisions. With intuition, you don't struggle with a decision—you *know* the solution.

We define intuition simply as a gut sense that you should or shouldn't do something.

When no decision seems right, intuition is telling you to put off a decision. Maybe you don't have enough information to make a decision, or the situation is going to change, thus changing your perspective and decision.

Your intuition is able to access and understand far more information than your conscious mind and senses can access. You sense intuition in your gut, in your heart,

and in your being. It will always tell you the right thing to do HERE. It is the beginning whispers of intelligence in your ear, the harmonious collaboration of mind, body, and brain. It always operates HERE.

○ You may sense intuition as a gut 'knowing', a strong pulsing in your emotional heart, or a strong thought such as, *DO IT!* Learn where you feel your intuition.

○ Intuition is your guide to living from your heart, not out of a conditioned, fearful response, or someone else's views. It cuts through any illusions you create, and is aligned with what is best for you and for everyone around you.

○ Intuition operates best when you are not afraid or stressed with racing thoughts, but are calm and quiet. Trusting that intuition will guide you down the best possible path can lessen anxiety in choices and decision-making.

If you don't follow your intuition due to fear, worry, or anxiety, it will increase your stress. Be true to your inner self, your wisdom, and your heart, and your life path will be easier.

Example:

I was trying to decide about an internet program to help market my writing and debated whether it was worth the fee. I actually filled out the form several times and deleted it. I felt crazy and neurotic, but finally paid for the program.

I downloaded the program on my computer and immediately realized it wasn't for me. I asked for a refund and received it.

It's funny now, but at the time I was reacting out of Self-Created Stress thoughts: *If I don't buy this program, I won't succeed! I will fail! I can't do this on my own!* These *What if?* thoughts caused me to second-guess my intuitive intelligence. They created the illusion that I would suffer harm if I didn't buy the program. That illusion—not my intuition—drove my action to buy the program.

My Self-Created Stress reactions blocked intuition, which was telling me that I didn't need the program. Intuition eventually triumphed over my fears, but my outlook and experience would have been more peaceful if I had trusted intuition immediately instead of following Self-Created Stress.

I learned what I needed to know about marketing from someone else for free. Even though I didn't see how my book could be successful then, it won an award. I succeeded without the internet program. Intuition was able to see that possibility immediately.

When you are afraid or stressed, the mind is preoccupied with these emotions. Intuition and your intelligence operate best with your senses fully alive, unrestricted by negative reactions.

Often someone else's intuition is the best course of action for *everyone involved*. For example, if a woman says to a man (or vice versa), (*My intuition says) I don't feel that you're a good match for me,* her intuition is best for her *and him.*

If you were in this situation, instead of fighting or reacting negatively to the woman's intuition with, *She doesn't like me! I'm not good enough! I'll never meet someone! She's stupid!* honor it and thank her for it. Because her intuition (or yours) will be best for you too, preventing you both from wasting energy in a doomed relationship. If it's just a timing issue, the opportunity may come around again when you next meet.

Ending Self-Created Stress allows intuition to operate fully. Learning to trust that inner sense of what to do can reduce Self-Created Stress reactions in any situation.

TRY THIS

1) When you are afraid, stressed, or confused by Self-Created Stress, take a few deep breaths, calm your thoughts, and ask yourself, *What is the best action for me*

to take HERE? You can ask this question multiple ways in regard to specific people, names, and events.

Listen to your mind intently in silence

This is similar to when we ask ourselves, *What was that person's name?*

We listen for a few moments in silence without trying to answer our question with thoughts. Our mind and brain continue to work on our question until—voila! Sooner or later your mind and brain provide the forgotten name!

This kind of questioning and listening for answers will work in all important areas of your life. Be patient.

If you don't get a clear answer, you need more information. The more you practice, the better you will become at trusting your own answers in life.

When you ask a question, *forget about what you know or think you know.* If you answer the question with your intellect and knowledge, you shut down the brain's amazing ability to find creative solutions and answers. Ask your question three times a day, for a month if need be, and focus on the question intently.

This process also works best if the questions are specific, such as, *Why do I react negatively to George when he asks me questions about my family?* Questions such as, *Why is the sky blue?* or *Why are cows brown?* are impossible for the brain to answer without a scientific explanation!

Answers to questions we ask ourselves often come when we least expect them, while walking, taking a shower, or doing some other activity. Taking a break from the intensity of our question allows the brain the space it needs to find the answer.

Let intuition be your guide. It connects you to everyone and everything with more information than your thoughts can ever give you.

PAUSE HERE TO ASK YOURSELF A SPECIFIC QUESTION ABOUT SOME ASPECT OF YOURSELF OR A RELATIONSHIP THAT YOU ARE NOT CLEAR ABOUT. LISTEN IN SILENCE WITHOUT TRYING TO ANSWER IT.

PRACTICE

1) A) Think of the last three times you struggled over a decision. It doesn't matter if the decisions were over small issues.

B) Think of the Self-Created Stress statements you created which resulted in worry over making the decisions in (A).

C) Create 1-2 playful exaggerations about the decision.

D) Say, think, & visualize the playful exaggerations, and smile!

Example 1:

A1) Decision: *Should I ask Mary/Bill out on a date?*

B) Self-Created Stress: *They'll say no. What's the point? They'll think I'm boring.*

C) Playful Exaggerations:

S/he will fall asleep out of boredom when s/he looks into my eyes!
If s/he says no, I will never be able to ask anyone out for a date again for eternity!

D) Say, think, & visualize the playful exaggerations, and smile!

Example 2:

A1) Decision: *What movie should I watch tonight?*

B)   Self-Created Stress: *I might not like it. The others won't like my choice. It will be a waste of time.*

C)   Playful Exaggerations:

> *I will turn to stone watching this movie!*
> *Once I turn the movie on, I won't be able to turn it off!*

D)   Say, think, & visualize the playful exaggerations, and smile!

PAUSE HERE TO CONSIDER THREE RECENT DECISIONS, ANY SELF-CREATED STRESS REACTIONS, AND A PLAYFUL EXAGGERATION.

A1) Decision:

_____

B) Self-Created Stress:

_____

C) Playful Exaggeration:

_____

Say, think, & visualize the playful exaggeration, and smile!

A2) Decision:

_____

B) Self-Created Stress:

_____

C) Playful Exaggeration:

_____

Say, think, & visualize the playful exaggeration, and smile!

A3) Decision:

_____

B) Self-Created Stress:

_____

C) Playful Exaggeration:

_____

Say, think, & visualize the playful exaggeration, and smile!

~

In each **Decision above**, did you have a gut sense of what to do, even though you were worried?

A1. Yes   No   A2. Yes   No   A3. Yes   No

In each case, did your decision turn out okay, even with the Self-Created Stress worries?

A1. Yes   No   A2. Yes   No   A3. Yes   No

In each case, did the Self-Created Stress make your decision harder and less fun?

A1. Yes   No   A2. Yes   No   A3. Yes   No

The purpose of this exercise is to separate intuition from worry, fear, or panic as a result of Self-Created Stress. Once you understand this, your intuition will short-circuit Self-Created Stress worries, fears, and illusions, and keep you calm on your path of action.

Many small decisions you make won't change your life for better or worse; a wrong movie choice doesn't matter. Even the possibility of someone saying *No* to a date is nothing to worry about. What matters most is remaining calm and peaceful, and enjoying the situation or action.

Trust that you can be calm no matter what. Use the question, *Did I remain calm?* as the benchmark for judging your success, instead of worrying over the results of your actions.

~

Note 1: In a very simplistic sense, intelligence is intuition operating in every action you take, wherever you are. Intuition is a good beginning point to understand intelligence.

~

Note 2: Even when you use intuition, seek out as much information as possible. I went through a long-term, severe autoimmune disease. I consulted over 100 doctors and alternative health practitioners. I was also told by many doctors who were experts and specialists in their field to "live with it" and "it can't be healed." Intuition said otherwise, so I kept looking until I found a cure. It ended up requiring a blend of supplements, allergy drops, a parasite pill, and energy exercises to reduce my symptoms by over 90%, and the remaining 10% is fading fast. Listen to everyone, but trust yourself!

~

THE TO-DO LIST

All you ever have is HERE & ONE action at a time.

The To-Do list is a useful tool for keeping ourselves organized in a complicated life. It's a mental or written list of reminders of what we need to do. But To-Do lists can trigger Self-Created Stress. Let's use our intuition to make the To-Do list an ally instead of an enemy.

In the past, To-Do lists organized me, but they also created stress and worry: *What should I do next? What if I can't get all of this done? I'm not moving fast enough!* The To-Do list never ended, because finished items were immediately replaced with new ones.

Taking on too many things in life results in stress. You lose time to relax, something all of us need daily. The U.S. model of working five days a week for 40+ hours, plus transportation time, leaves only two days a week to run errands, have fun, and take care of necessities. It is a stressful model other parts of the world have wisely walked away from.

Even if we have enough time to get things done, too many of us carry the To-Do list in our head, driving us forward to the next thing on the list like a hamster running on a never-ending wheel.

Self-Created Stress might be a silent tape of messages running in your thoughts without you even being aware of it. You are rejecting HERE with: *I won't/can't be calm, happy, or fulfilled until the To-Do list is finished.*

The illusion we create is that we are in danger or will suffer harm (even if the harm is a lack of fulfillment) if we don't finish the To-Do list.

These types of responses are negative reactions to an observable FACT, which is our To-Do list.

But what if, out of necessity, you *have* to complete every item on the To-Do list? What if you're a single parent with two kids and a long To-Do list that must be finished?

What if you have a nonstop stressful job where the To-Do list is never finished, and you lay awake at night worrying about it? What if you spend every Sunday night worrying about returning to work on Monday?

Is there a way to end the To-Do list stress, other than taking a vacation, death, a health breakdown, or retirement? Can you be busy and efficient without engaging in Self-Created Stress at all?

When I began marketing my books, my To-Do list was endless stress. Now it's simply a list, and intuition peacefully guides me along the way through it.

TRY THIS

1) Use your intuition. If you are staring wearily at a long To-Do list, interrupt any Self-Created Stress statements, and instead ask yourself: *What should I do first?*

    Listen for the answer out of intuition, not worry or fear created by Self-Created Stress. Pay attention, and in time you will find yourself knowing what to do, what can be let go, and what isn't worth doing or worrying about HERE.

To practice, write down in any order of priority what you consider to be your current To-Do list. This could be for your home life, school tasks, or at your job.

Example:

laundry   oil change   haircut   walk the dog   call a friend
organize basement   homework   bike maintenance

_____   _____   _____

_____   _____   _____

_____   _____   _____

_____   _____   _____

Let your eyes run over your list. Smile while you do this, take a few breaths if you need to calm yourself, and ask your intuitive self:

A) Do I need to do any of these IMMEDIATELY? **Circle or mentally note those**.

B) Which of these absolutely MUST be done in the next 24 hours? **Write 1 by them.**

C) Which of these absolutely MUST be done in the next 3 days? **Write 3 by them**.

D) Which of these absolutely MUST be done in the next week? **Write 7 by them**.

Any items on the list that are not circled or don't have a number probably don't belong on the list. A better place for them might be on a calendar to let you know when to put them on the list.

This exercise is designed to give you confidence in approaching your To-Do list with calm and intelligence. Make your To-Do list your friend and ally instead of the enemy.

2) When you notice Self-Created Stress thoughts about what you have to get done, interrupt them and playfully exaggerate the neurotic racing of the mind. It will help you put the To-Do list into perspective.

   Examples of playful exaggerations:

   *My body will blow up like a hot air balloon
   if I don't finish my To-Do list!
   The world clock will stop if my To-Do list
   doesn't get finished today!*

3) When your To-Do list seems overwhelming or stressful, tell yourself one truth; ***I can only do one thing HERE, not the whole list at once, so I might as well relax with each task as I do it and enjoy it.***

   Also remind yourself, *My goal is to remain calm, even while working on my To-Do list.*

4) When you feel in a hurry and stressed, use playful substitutions for the task or the location you are going to (this is covered in more depth in Chapter 14).

Again, by using playful exaggerations, you

○ interrupt the rote response of the brain,

○ tell it you're no longer interested in that response,

○ no longer believe the negative response is a *fact*, and

○ reject the negative rote neural pattern and inform the brain you want it to change.

This may sound simplistic, yet it works!

~

Example 1:

If you're in a hurry and stressed to get to the grocery store, interrupt the thought process and make playful substitutions for *grocery store*.

I have to get to the desert! To the ocean! To the mountains!

Example 2:

If you are responding with Self-Created Stress over having to make a dessert for a dinner party, interrupt your thoughts and make playful substitutions for *make a dessert*.

I must swim down the Nile River for the dinner party! I have to climb Mount Everest for the dinner party!

You are reminding the brain that rote neural responses, and the resultant stress, are no longer acceptable. The brain will listen, and it will change. Master vs. Servant.

PAUSE HERE TO CREATE PLAYFUL EXAGGERATIONS FOR THREE TASKS ON A TO-DO LIST THAT YOU HAVE REACTED TO WITH SELF-CREATED STRESS.

A) Task:

_____

B)   Playful Exaggeration:

_____

Say, think, & visualize the playful exaggeration, and smile!

C)   Task:

_____

D)   Playful Exaggeration:

_____

Say, think, & visualize the playful exaggeration, and smile!

E)   Task:

_____

F)   Playful Exaggeration:

_____

Say, think, & visualize the playful exaggeration, and smile!

~

FURTHER STEPS TO REDUCE TO-DO LIST STRESS IN THE SHORT TERM

1)   Take on less if you can! Look at your list and cross off anything that isn't essential.

2)   Give yourself time to breathe deeply. Literally. Three times a day (or whenever you are stressed), breathe in, hold your breath for 2-4 seconds, then exhale slowly. Focus on the air going in and out. A half-dozen times is enough to relax the brain.

3) If you find yourself endlessly racing to organized events for your children, remember that children benefit more from spending time with rested and relaxed parents. Simple activities like cooking together, reading a favorite book, or going for a family walk provide positive results. You are also modeling to your children how to relax and remain calm.

4) Remember, some things on the To-Do list don't need perfection, like cleaning the house or folding laundry (unless you enjoy these tasks and they help you relax).

5) Singing your To-Do list out loud is another great way to bring humor to your overworked mind and is great for brain chemistry. *First I have to do the laundry, then I must do the cleaning, homework next, shop for groceries, and fix the car...* Sing it and smile. Be HERE. Have fun, despite the list.

PAUSE HERE AND DO THIS NOW; SING YOUR TO-DO LIST.

6) Set a goal of rewarding yourself with a break from the list after you finish part of it.

7) Every day, no matter how much you may be rushing around, whether at work or home, take at least a few minutes to stop, stand outside, and watch clouds and birds or listen to the wind in the trees. Allow the beauty of nature to inspire you.

PAUSE HERE AND DO THIS NOW (OBSERVE NATURE).

CHAPTER 7

Strong Self-Created Stress Reactions & Trauma

What should you do if you are caught up in strong negative reactions?

W hat happens if you are caught up in a strong Self-Created Stress reaction that you can't interrupt or end? What if the patterned neural pathways you created are so strong that you obsessively keep repeating them? What if the emotions associated with the reactions are so overwhelming that you cannot slow them down, weaken them, or change them as they occur?

The illusions associated with these emotions are equally strong.

Whenever we have strong, overpowering reactions, there are underlying thought patterns slipping in that trigger our emotions. You have to address them so you are not overwhelmed and repeating the same emotional reactions and illusions that enslave you.

Remember, every time you react emotionally with a strong rote reaction, you are strengthening that neural wiring in the brain. This also strengthens the brain's mechanical response. It becomes a vicious circle of reinforced repetition, rote response, reinforced repetition, rote response, etc.

When we're reliving an illusion of a past event, we feel as if we are in serious danger HERE, even if it isn't true. The illusion of danger may feel so real that we cannot immediately escape it.

What do you do then?

1) As soon as you can, get out of the situation. Go for a nature walk, swim, exercise, do deep breathing, or take a cold or warm shower.

2) When you are calm, sit down and write about the event. If your reactions were triggered by a specific person, thought, or situation, write down why you think you reacted the way you did. If you're not sure, use the information in the previous chapter about *Intuition*, and ask yourself, *Why did I react the way I did?*

Make this question as specific as possible by using names of people, the event, any triggers you can think of, and the resulting emotions you felt. Feel free to ask yourself questions in multiple ways.

If you still don't find an answer, don't worry about it. If the person or situation presents an actual physical threat, then you have to get help. But if the threat is just the product of a past event, focus on making it absurd.

3) Create playful exaggerations about your reaction to the person and/or the event. Next say, think, & visualize these exaggerations, and smile.

Example:

Let's say the trigger event is speaking in front of a group, made worse by a critical supervisor who always sits in the front row. You sweat, you feel fear, you freeze up inside, and your lips feel numb. Even if your reaction isn't this bad, perhaps you can't wait for the event to be over.

Write down several playful exaggerations, such as:

I am going to melt like ice cream in front of this crowd!
or
My sweat will form a small puddle around my shoes!

If your exaggerations bring a smile to your face, you are on the right track. If not, smile and continue anyway.

For the critical supervisor watching your speech, you can add,

S/he will take out an ad in the New York Times about how bad my presentation was!

The next time you have to give a presentation, repeat these exaggerations the day before, and leading up to it. Smile as you walk up to the stage. Smile at the audience. The goal is to interrupt your rote thought patterns, replace them with exaggerations, and smile. You are telling the brain, *I reject this rote neural response!* The brain will listen, and it will change.

As the saying goes, *Rome wasn't built in a day,* so give yourself time to end this pattern. It will end because you are leaving the brain no choice!

TRY THIS

1) A) Write down situations or people for which you have very strong reactions.

B) Write down playful exaggerations about these situations or people

C) Say them out loud, think them, visualize, and smile!

Example (from earlier):

A)   Strong reaction: *I'm terrified of giving my speech in front of a crowd and my supervisor!*

B)   Playful Exaggeration: *I'm going to float up like a balloon in front of everyone!* or *My supervisor looks like my favorite teddy bear!*

A)   Strong Reaction:

_____

B)   Playful Exaggeration:

_____

Say, think, & visualize the playful exaggeration, and smile!

A)   Strong Reaction:

_____

B)   Playful Exaggeration:

_____

Say, think, & visualize the playful exaggeration, and smile!

A)   Strong Reaction:

_____

B)   Playful Exaggeration:

_____

Say, think, & visualize the playful exaggeration, and smile!

~

TRAUMATIC EXPERIENCES, EVENTS, OR PEOPLE

When I was seven years old, I was traumatized by a move that didn't bother my older brother or younger sister. After that I was afraid of any change or transition. In high school I was bullied, and in my late twenties I was hit by a long-term, painful severe illness that resulted in financial ruin. It is now behind me.

But those experiences gave me:

○ a deep passion for looking inwardly for solutions, which resulted in *living with intelligence HERE*, and

○ empathy for anyone suffering from trauma.

I wouldn't trade my experiences for anything; they helped make me who I am. Yet we don't want to continue creating pain from past traumas, nor allow them to dictate our responses to life HERE.

More Examples of Trauma

A friend of mine has always been afraid of Minnesota nonpoisonous garter snakes. The snakes are most certainly more afraid of her.

Another friend never wants to go into freshwater lakes. When she was younger, she discovered a dead man floating nearby beneath a dock. The vast majority of lakes are without dead bodies, yet she still responds with anxiety to lakes as if she might find one, and she avoids swimming in them.

Perhaps your father yelled at you often, or a friend/spouse betrayed you.

Many of us have some kind of trauma or deeper fears that often began in childhood. Instead of living HERE, we are replaying past events (See Chapter 14). We create an illusion that feels as if we're still back at that moment, still seeing and experiencing the past event.

What do we do about this?

Psychoanalysis, therapy, biofeedback, CBT (cognitive behavioral therapy), meditation, etc. are all approaches that can ease traumatic events. Some physically traumatic events (assault, beatings, abuse) may require the help of other professionals to stop retraumatizing ourselves.

However, for many lesser traumas we can challenge and play with the current thought patterns that are the residual effect of our trauma.

TRY THIS

A) Write down a past trauma.

B) Next write down the effects of the past trauma and Self-Created Stress thoughts associated with it.

C) Then write down playful exaggerations of the past event, and of your current thoughts related to it.

D) Lastly Say, think, & visualize the playful exaggeration, and smile!

Example:

For my trauma after the age seven move, I could write down:

1) Trauma: *The move at age seven scared me.*

2) Results/thoughts: *It made me scared of change and less trusting of myself.* One underlying belief was: *Change will always be horrible.*

3) Playful Exaggeration: *The move turned me into a frog!* or *Change will make my hair stand straight up on my head!"*

The idea is not to trivialize fears or traumas, but to end the repetitive neural patterns that continue to replay the trauma and associated pain.

PAUSE HERE TO WRITE DOWN THREE TRAUMAS YOU HAD IN THE PAST, RESULTING THOUGHTS OR BELIEFS, AND A PLAYFUL EXAGGERATION.

If you don't have three, don't make them up! If your traumas seem much smaller than someone else's, still write them down, because they are important for you!

A) Trauma:

_____

B) Result/Thoughts/Underlying Belief:

_____

C) Playful Exaggeration:

_____

Say, think, & visualize the playful exaggeration, and smile!

A) Trauma:

_____

B) Result/Thoughts/Underlying Belief:

_____

C) Playful Exaggeration:

_____

Say, think, & visualize the playful exaggeration, and smile!

A)   Trauma:

_____

B)   Result/Thoughts/Underlying Belief:

_____

C)   Playful Exaggeration:

_____

Say, think, & visualize the playful exaggeration, and smile!

PRACTICE

1)   Another way to get at trauma is to visualize the past event differently. For my traumatic seven-year-old-move, I can visualize myself remaining calm, and talking to my parents. I can see myself entering the new classroom at the new school with calm and confidence. Feel the emotions of calm and confidence. Humor and smiles always help in reimagining such events. It changes the 'seriousness' of the past reaction and allows the brain to let it go.

Again, this is not to make light of serious physical abuse or terrifying, life-or-death trauma. But it is a way to help your brain let go of the repetitive thoughts that are still traumatizing you, even though the event is long gone.

PRACTICE THIS NOW. RE-VISUALIZE ONE TRAUMATIC SITUATION IN YOUR LIFE TO SEE, FEEL, AND EXPERIENCE IT DIFFERENTLY.

The more you playfully exaggerate and smile about traumatic events, the less strength the brain's related neural pattern has when you encounter situations that trigger the old trauma. It will be easier to interrupt the reaction, be more objective and aware, and less reactive to it.

This exercise is also useful for current traumas we face such as COVID-19 concerns, health issues, loss of a job, isolation, divorce, etc. We're conditioned by every form of media in society that it is normal to respond with internal pain or trauma to adverse or challenging events. We often believe this is a true fact about life. It isn't.

As you continue with the techniques in this book, you will begin to see that events, people, and situations do not *make you afraid or stressed*. Your own thoughts and Self-Created Stress reactions do.

Your reactions to your thoughts = fear, worry, anxiety, anger, disappointment, loneliness, and sadness. We are creating these inside our brains.

Luckily you can end the old rote neural pathways and replace them with new responses based on HERE. You can rewire your brain. Master vs. Servant.

CHAPTER 8

Goals & Visualization, Acceptance, & Expect the Unexpected

You can do anything if you accept the results.

Everything we do is, at some level, an attempt to be happy. The way we often approach this is by thinking, *If I can just get to this goal, buy this, do this, or achieve this, then I will be happy!* These are illusions, not facts! And these illusions are part of the neural net responses that we are going to change.

Advertisements often imply that our happiness depends on acquiring things such as new cars, the 'best' vacations, the latest tech, a mansion, etc. The illusion we create for ourselves is that happiness HERE is at risk if we don't reach these goals. That very belief causes stress.

If we believe that our happiness is dependent on attaining a goal, then when we reach any desired goal or activity, our mind often moves on to the next goal in a never-ending search for happiness. This Self-Created Stress never arrives at happiness.

Ironically, we don't have to "get" anywhere to be happy. It's HERE. And it's only HERE.

Happiness is being content with wherever we are, even while pursuing goals or activities. It is savoring each raindrop. This doesn't mean accepting horrible or mediocre situations without trying to change them. But it does mean we want to end Self-Created Stress as much as possible, no matter where we are, even while putting effort into changing our lives.

Also, if you react to a personal goal or activity with Self-Created Stress statements such as: *I can't do it; It's too hard/scary;* or *It's impossible,* you limit yourself. You allow Self-Created Stress illusions to determine your course of action.

I'm not talking about bungee jumping. I also don't want to free-climb mountains without safety ropes.

But if you dismiss worthwhile challenges and goals out of fear or Self-Created Stress reactions, you may never find out what you are capable of gaining. You could learn how to cook a complicated (or simple) meal, design a website, lose weight, or learn how to sail.

Limiting yourself through negative thoughts is another Self-Created Stress situation. Denying yourself what you yearn for leads to unhappiness, a lack of fulfillment, and stress. Even if you're not aware of self-imposed limits, they still cause pain.

~

Example 1:

When I was younger, I dreamed of studying with a true kung fu master. And I found a world-class Vietnamese kung fu master at the local YMCA who agreed to teach me!

When I first began practicing kung fu, I practiced up to four hours a day, every day. After a few months it became less fun, more difficult, and stressful.

I asked myself, *Why don't I enjoy this anymore?*

I realized that I was fixated on attaining a black belt, a goal that would take five years and felt impossible. I was focused on the endpoint instead of HERE. My running background Self-Created Stress tape was, *I will never get a black belt. It's impossible, too hard, I'm not good enough.* This wasn't FACT, but I reacted as if it was. I accepted the illusion that I was incapable of ever acquiring a black belt, which deflated all of my energy HERE.

This resulted in a negative emotional reaction to my workouts, driven by thoughts such as: *If I'm not going to get a black belt, why bother?*

I told myself, *Change your viewpoint or quit.* I decided to just enjoy the workouts. I ended my belief in Self-Created Stress statements about my inability to obtain a black belt, and thus I ended the illusion I had created from those statements.

Practice became easy and something I looked forward to again, and I eventually earned a black belt. Earning the black belt wasn't the huge event I had imagined, but just another step in the process of learning kung fu HERE and having fun.

That shift, focusing on HERE instead of a far-off goal, made the goal attainable, put it in perspective, and gave me the strength and wisdom necessary to endure many other challenges in life.

Example 2:

Let's say you want to lose weight. You've tried diets, strategies, and exercise programs with no success. You feel frustrated, hopeless, and have given up. Losing 15, 50, or 100 pounds feels like a mountain you can't climb.

Try to operate your goal from HERE. Instead of believing the illusions created by thoughts such as, *I can't lose 15, 50, 100 pounds! It's impossible! I've tried! It's too hard!* start with, *I will begin HERE with this meal.* Tell yourself; *I will eat healthy, take smaller portions, take small mouthfuls, chew slowly, put my fork or spoon down between bites, and pay attention to my body and stomach so I can hear my body when it says, "I'm full, stop eating!"*

I used the exact above strategy in high school when I was overweight due to emotional issues related to being bullied. It also helps to use a small fork or spoon, such as an olive fork or condiment spoon. It took many months to lose the weight, but I did it ONE MEAL at a time, paying attention HERE, not listening to Self-Created Stress statements of *I can't succeed,* etc.

Many diet plans and exercise programs fail because the participants are focused on *endpoint*, instead of HERE. To live HERE is to be aware and mindful, and free of chasing illusions.

When you believe limiting statements about your abilities, you're telling the brain, *Stop trying to make me better in this activity, there's no point, it's unattainable!* You are wiring the brain to STOP PURSUING THIS. The brain listens to everything you tell it, directly or indirectly, and it will stop working to find ways for you to succeed. Worse, you are ignoring your emotional heart and creating stress.

You cannot find and pursue your passions, or accomplish your goals, if you tell yourself you are not capable, not worthy, or focus on how good you have to be. Pursue whatever excites you HERE, and life will be a blast.

One point worth noting again: If you're not sure why you feel a certain way, or what Self-Created Stress tape might be playing in the background of your thoughts, ask yourself questions! Make the questions specific and clear. Listen in silence for the answer. The brain won't stop working until it brings you one. (See Chapter 6)

Your brain is the most sophisticated computer on the planet. Program in the right question, and it will keep working until it finds the answer. The more you do this, the easier it becomes to find answers.

Talking to friends or a counselor might help you see the answer sooner, but sometimes those options are not readily available. Finding a good counselor to help you can also be a challenge. The good news is, you can become your own best super-counselor.

VISUALIZE YOUR GOALS AS IF THEY ARE HERE

Olympic athletes have been doing this for many decades:

A) they visualize themselves running or competing successfully in their event, and/or

B) they visualize themselves standing on the podium with a gold medal. Obviously they have to train like crazy too.

You can also visualize your life, your goals, your dreams. You can actively create them! This means you set your mind, body, brain, and connections to everything to order up the life and experiences you want. As stated earlier, I wanted to train with a real kung fu master. I thought about it, visualized it, and then met one at a local YMCA and did it! And this was when I knew nothing about the visualization process—so I certainly wasn't an expert at it.

When I was traveling in the South Pacific for over a year, everyone asked me, *What are you going to do when you get to Australia?* I was running out of money and didn't know anyone in Australia. My answer: *I'm going to train to be a massage therapist and earn money from that so I can live a block off Bondi Beach.* I visualized that result. I made it a reality. It happened.

I met a woman on Bondi Beach, told her my dream, and she knew the owner of the main massage clinic in Sydney (Double Bay Massage). I was able to walk in and get trained and employed there! And I lived a block off the Bondi Beach.

That doesn't mean you visualize, *I will win the gold medal at the Olympics in the 100-meter dash,* and then expect to do so with no training, no skill, no coach, or no effort. But there are many things, like my assertion of, *I will be a massage therapist*, that don't require anything more than visualizing it.

I visualized *movie deals* for my thriller books. It happened! But I also reached out to eighty producers with queries on my books.

You can use visualization for any goals or even life-changing events. For example, in the last chapter we discussed being fearful of giving a speech. Perhaps your goal is to enjoy giving speeches in front of large audiences. Visualize yourself giving a speech, smiling, being relaxed, and everyone clapping loudly when you finish. You need only spend seconds to a minute doing this.

Practice visualizing, and you will get better at it and feel confident that you have the power to determine the course of your life.

When you visualize a reality you desire, the brain, body, and mind all focus on creating that reality—you are engaging the whole universe, and it will respond. You are creating your life instead of being a victim to it.

TRY THIS

What dreams do you have? What goals? To meet the love of your life? To live in a nice apartment or home by a lake? To be an author? To get a certain job? To learn a certain skill? Visualize the endpoint of you having attained that goal HERE. See yourself in the apartment or house looking out at the lake. Or see yourself introducing 'the love of your life' to your family and friends. Be creative, be specific with details, and hold it dear. Smile. Feel what it will be like to have it. Exciting! Fulfilling! Follow your heart!

Write down and visualize the specifics of three dreams or events now.

1) _____

2) _____

3) _____

~

THE POWER OF YET

When you talk about where you are in pursuing a goal, use the word *Yet*. For example, I'm only selling 25 books/day, and my goal is *to sell 100+ books/day*. Whenever I talk to others or myself, the spoken or thought message is, *I haven't reached my goal, YET. But I will!* That keeps the door open and doesn't stop the brain's efforts toward the goal. The brain hears my INTENT and it's full steam ahead to find a way to do it!

Martin Luther King and Gandhi certainly had doubts along the way, but that didn't stop them from changing a whole country. They might have had Self-Created Stress doubts such as, *It's impossible! Why bother? I can't do it!* But they ignored the illusions those statements presented. Their INTENT was to attain their goal, no matter what.

If a goal is worthwhile, go for it. Then you won't live with regrets. You may have a gift the world needs, or something that brings great joy to you or others. End believing and following Self-Created Stress statements and you will have no limits.

TRY THIS

Take a moment now to think of goals you might have considered, but stopped pursuing due to Self-Created Stress statements. Then restate any Self-Created Stress reactions that have limited your choices:

Example 1:

If you think, *I can't be a good basketball player.*

Change that statement to, *I will shoot hoops and have fun no matter how good I am, and keep improving.*

Example 2:

If you think, *This food is great! I could never cook like this.*

Change that statement to, *I can learn how to cook great food too. I'll take classes, watch cooking shows, or ask someone who has a tasty recipe to help me improve my ability.*

Consider any Self-Created Stress thoughts that make a goal or activity seem difficult or impossible, or take away your ability to fully enjoy your efforts. This includes thinking, *I can't change my Self-Created Stress patterns!*

Restate your Self-Created Stress thoughts to a positive affirmation of doing whatever you can HERE. Focus on enjoying whatever level of skill you bring to an activity or goal.

PRACTICE

1) As you become aware of Self-Created Stress statements that you tell yourself about goals you find appealing, change them!

A) If you think, *I can never learn to*
_____ *(fill in the blank)*
Change it to, *I can get better at* _____
(fill in the blank), and I will pursue it because it makes me feel good.

B) If you think, *I'm not good enough, smart enough to, capable of* _____ *(fill in the blank)*
Change it to, *I can get better at* _____
(fill in the blank), even if it takes me longer than others.

C) If you think, *I'm too old/not old enough to*_____ *(fill in the blank)*
Change it to, *My age is not a barrier. I will pursue*
_____ *(fill in the blank), because it makes me happy and fulfilled, regardless of my age.*

PAUSE HERE TO CONSIDER SMALL OR BIG GOALS YOU MIGHT WANT TO PURSUE (OR ARE CURRENTLY PURSUING) & POSITIVELY REPHRASE HOW YOU LOOK AT THEM.

A) _____

B) _____

C) _____

2) Watch YouTube videos or read books to learn how to do something new. I do it all the time. Start slow. Learning something new can feel awkward at first. Give it a chance. And listen to your heart, not your Self-Created Stress thoughts. If an activity brings you joy, keep going.

3) Use playful exaggerations when you block yourself from goals.

~

Example:

If you think, *Only brilliant superstar people can succeed like that!*

Change it to, *Only people with dragon tattoos on their butts can do that!* or *Only ducks with purple beaks can do that!*

The idea again is to interrupt, change, and laugh at the silliness of allowing a rote, dead reaction to decide your course of action.

Many people have learned skills very late in life. Some writers publish best-selling books in their nineties. I've often heard young people and students I work with say, *I can never do that*, even when they have great aptitude for the very thing they concluded is impossible. When individuals believe a self-imposed limit (an illusion), they are looking at the *endpoint*, not the journey, and not HERE.

Give yourself permission to try and enjoy your effort. Give it time. Anything worthwhile is worth spending as much time as it takes. You may never be a "superstar," but if you are enjoying yourself, you will be smiling and have a star-like quality. That is the goal.

EXPECTATIONS CREATE DISAPPOINTMENT

Recently I waited in a packed shoe store where the clerks were all busy. I wanted new sandals. I thought how lucky I was that I could afford them, and that the store had the ones I wanted.

While I waited, several customers grumbled over the slow service. The longest any of us waited was fifteen minutes. Expecting faster service, one disgruntled customer left the store. When I lived in Fiji, customer service sometimes took a week!

If we operate out of the belief that life should move along the way we want and expect it to, Self-Created Stress produces a world of disappointment. This is just another form of stress and another form of self-inflicted pain. Life isn't what we want it to be.

If you accept a long wait in a service line, you can still enjoy observing your reactions, doing a body scan, or talking to others.

Acceptance allows you to create a world of harmony, even when faced with an obstacle or unmet expectation. You can choose to be calm and at peace, and bring something positive to the event. Create the world you want instead of reacting to the world you don't want.

Life *is* the unexpected and unknown, including our relationships with imperfect people; and all of us are imperfect. No one knows what the next day will bring. Life is unpredictable.

If you believe your happiness is dependent on the millions of things that are often out of your control (a football game score, a rainy day, etc.), your peace of mind becomes unpredictable too. If you give anyone, or any event, power over your happiness and well-being, there is no psychological security. To have psychological security, we need to remain calm, which means we need to end internal conflict or greatly minimize it. We need to end or greatly reduce Self-Created Stress, including disappointment and expectations.

Why does one person remain calm or happy on a rainy day or in rush hour traffic, while someone else finds the situation miserable? As in weightlifting, mathematics, music, or any other skill, everyone has different natural abilities due to upbringing or genetics.

One large study of 1,300 sets of identical and fraternal twins at the University of Minnesota estimated that as much as 50% of happiness is pre-wired into our brains through genetics. Thus some of us are genetically wired from birth to be happier and more cheerful than others.[10]

We may learn negative responses from our parents, friends, family members, or the news media that someone else does not. Some people perhaps had a traumatic event when younger and still play out that trauma and stress on a daily basis. Whatever reasons that have led to your own Self-Created Stress, it is up to you to end it.

Every situation or obstacle you face is an opportunity to see yourself—your rote neural programming—and change.

End expectations and assumptions. Instead, see and be alert to what is HERE.

TRY THIS

It's important to remember your *intent* is to interrupt the old neural patterns in your brain—your rote thoughts—and thus change how you respond to situations. Every time you change your thought pattern or interrupt old thought responses, you are changing your brain. Keep your intent in your heart. You are changing the brain's old neural net, the old reactions, to create a new neural net. You are the Master, forcing the brain to rewire itself.

1) Playfully exaggerate any of your Self-Created Stress reactions related to disappointment.

Example:

If you're thinking, *What a long line! I expected it to be short today. I hate standing in line!*

Interrupt it and say or think,

> *I will need to go into the emergency room on Mars*
> *to cure myself of this cursed line!*

Or whisper,

> *I will be standing in this line so long that I will*
> *miss my next two birthdays!*

Any ridiculous, silly, or humorous statement works to minimize your harsh reaction. Visualize the images of the playful exaggerations. Smile.

Instead of clinging to the old mature thoughts that interfere with your happiness, allow your childlike playfulness to flower. You can use videos, cartoons, movies, books, or any other story to pull out images and humor for the playful exaggerations.

PRACTICE

1) End disappointment by:

A) Think of three recent disappointments, regardless of how small or big they were.

B) Rephrase your disappointment with a playful exaggeration by substituting silly words for yourself and the other person, object, or situation.

C) Say, think, & visualize the playful exaggeration, and smile!

A) Disappointment:

_____

B) Playful Exaggeration:

_____

Say, think, & visualize the playful exaggeration, and smile!

A)   Disappointment:

_____

B)   Playful Exaggeration:

_____

Say, think, & visualize the playful exaggeration, and smile!

A)   Disappointment:

_____

B)   Playful Exaggeration:

_____

Say, think, & visualize the playful exaggeration, and smile!

~

Note: Another variation on disappointment is created when we think or say, *I miss when we used to* _____ or *I miss* _____ or *I miss that* _____ (fill in the blanks).

If there is something you wish you were still doing, then do it, or find new friends to do it with you. Don't give power and life to images (memories) that make you feel your life is *less than it used to be*; less fulfilling, less happy, or less exciting. This is a form of self-inflicted pain. Let the "past" go, follow your heart HERE, and find out what will fulfill it HERE. You can also use playful exaggerations when you find yourself using these statements. E.g., *I miss all the times I stubbed my big toe!*

~

EMBRACE THE UNPREDICTABLE REALITY OF LIFE

Pay attention to the unpredictable nature of life and see if you can accept it. When faced with the unexpected, take a deep breath—or three—to reset any reactions from Self-Created Stress, and remind yourself:

○ *Life is the unexpected.*

○ *I will expect the unexpected.*

○ *I will find calm and beauty in the unexpected.*

○ *I will create the beautiful world I want, even in unexpected situations.*

Nothing will end Self-Created Stress faster than simply accepting things instead of fighting them internally.

TRY THIS

1) Think of three unpredictable or unexpected things that happened over the last days or weeks that you reacted to with Self-Created Stress. (E.g., a teacher or supervisor complained about your work; you lost your wallet; you twisted your ankle; the weather interfered with your plans, etc.)

A) _____

B) _____

C) _____

Remind yourself that unexpected and unpredictable events are a natural part of life.

2) Research shows that singing is calming and lessens stress. Group singing has an even stronger positive effect on brain chemistry.[11] It doesn't matter if you have a good voice. Sing someone else's song or create

your own happy, silly song and sing it daily wherever you feel comfortable. Do this for one month.

You may think, *Singing a made-up song is childish!* Childishness is reacting angrily or with frustration to events or people. True childlike qualities of wonder and playfulness are gifts we should embrace our whole lives.

Your lyrics can be simple; 3-4 lines you repeat are enough. For example: *I'm a lucky happy guy, I love the blue in the sky, I smile every day, because the birds sing away.* I'm sure you can do better. Rhyming isn't important; what matters is that the words make you feel good.

PAUSE HERE TO MAKE UP YOUR SONG NOW, AND THEN SING IT!

_____

_____

_____

_____

CHAPTER 9

Labels, Contradictions, & HERE

Labels blind us to what is in front of us.

L abels limit us and create illusions in our relationships with people, nature, and our senses. They are another form of Self-Created Stress.

If you think, *I don't like people who tell jokes!* you lump all people who tell jokes into the same pile despite their differences.

The thought, *I can't stand Jack!* reduces the individual, Jack, to one word (*Jack*) and past memories associated with him. It doesn't allow room for change in him, or yourself, or allow you to create a better, healthier relationship.

If you walk out your door thinking, *This is a lousy day!* and believe your words, you are allowing five words to define and capture your whole day.

It's impossible to define all the rich details our senses bring to us with a thousand words, let alone five. The illusion is that you believe you have captured and reduced your whole day to five words, thus allowing a dead, rote neural habit to blind you to your senses.

By reacting to people or situations with labels, you lose the opportunity to see something new HERE, in yourself or others, or in your surroundings. Your label limits your action to rote responses. Thus you lose the only adventure you have, which is HERE.

You may be wondering, *Is that all there is, just HERE? That seems so boring!*

It may feel exciting to have thoughts racing around, creating excitement through illusions that give us a sense of movement. But in reality, illusions cause stress, divide attention, and increase the potential for accidents and misery. Our planet and the current state of affairs is the result of 7.8+ billion people chasing their thoughts and illusions.

If you are living fully HERE, there is no boredom. Creativity, inner peace, and happiness will blossom. You are engaged with HERE like a happy child encountering life for the first time. Everything will feel new, exciting, and awesome!

TRY THIS

1) Notice labels that you create and play with them.

Examples: You could change the following labels:

○ Change *Management are idiots,* to *Everyone in the company is sometimes smart.*

○ Change *I hate dressing up,* to *I'm glad I have something to wear.*

○ Change *I hate meetings,* to *I will observe and learn from my reactions to people in the meeting.*

2) Notice the unique details in a weather pattern that you usually complain about.

3) Notice interesting or unique details of someone who rubs you the wrong way.

4)   When you find yourself repeating any negative or reactive Self-Created Stress label that you know you've said or thought before, say to yourself:

○ *This is a unique situation. I will pay attention.*

○ *This is a unique person. I will find something positive about them.*

○ *This is a unique activity or event, and I will do something new with it.*

Try it. It will change who you are.

PRACTICE

1)   A) Write down or think about words you use to label events, days, activities, or people that bother you. It could be; I hate *meetings*, I don't like *chatty people,* I don't like *Mary.*

B) Write down or think about what prompts that label.

C) Write or say something affirmative and unique about that day, event, or person.

D) Create a playful exaggeration for the label. Say, think, & visualize it. Smile.

These four steps will help you break down and end labels and allow you to find the uniqueness of every situation and person.

Example:

A)   Label: I hate *stressful Saturday mornings!*

B)   What prompts the label *stressful Saturday mornings?* Perhaps *because I have too many things to do on Saturday morning!*

C) Unique and positive details: *The sun is shining. I have a warm bed. Breakfast will be great. I can help my family.*

D) Playful Exaggeration: *Saturday mornings are so busy I don't have time to blink!*

PAUSE HERE TO THINK OF THREE LABELS YOU USE, WHAT PROMPTS THE LABEL, UNIQUE AND POSITIVE DETAILS, AND A PLAYFUL EXAGGERATION.

A) Label:

_____

B) What Prompts the Label:

_____

C) Unique & Positive Details about the Person, Place, or Event:

_____

D) Playful Exaggeration:

_____

Say, think, & visualize the playful exaggeration, and smile!

A) Label:

_____

B) What Prompts the Label:

_____

C) Unique & Positive Details about the Person, Place, or Event:

_____

D) Playful Exaggeration:

_____

Say, think, & visualize the playful exaggeration, and smile!

A) Label:

_____

B) What Prompts the Label:

_____

C) Unique & Positive Details about the Person, Place, or Event:

_____

D) Playful Exaggeration:

_____

Say, think, & visualize the playful exaggeration, and smile!

2) Research shows that gratitude for only three things daily can bring a sense of positivity into our lives and change brain chemistry. Keep a small gratitude journal by your bed. Every night, write down three specific things you are grateful for. Also do this in the morning when you get up. It can turn your mindset positive for the whole day.

Example for a gratitude journal entry:

I have a cool job. I tried my best today to organize my desk. I had a healthy lunch. I have a comfortable bed. I have clean clothing. I gained a new insight on ending stress.

○ The more specific you are, the more variety, the better.

○ Don't repeat the same things every time.

○ You can be grateful for *refrigeration, heat, fans, sun, moon, water, food, shoes, plates, silverware, buttons, zippers, friends, conversations, campfires, a specific piece of clothing, etc.* It's an endless list.

In time you'll end up feeling grateful all day long! Do this for thirty days, or a lifetime. This is especially helpful when you are stuck, frustrated, focusing on the negative, the glass half-empty, etc. Start listing the things you are thankful for, and it will put life in perspective.

PAUSE HERE TO THINK OF THREE THINGS THAT YOU ARE GRATEFUL FOR.

1) _____

2) _____

3) _____

~

STRESS AND CONTRADICTIONS IN THE BRAIN

You can only be HERE

With the thought process, our brain creates contradictions that end up creating illusions = Self-Created Stress. We've talked about this already, but let's go into it again a little more carefully.

It's easy to understand when we wake up that our dreams are fantasy and didn't actually happen in real life. Yet dreams often mirror our daytime Self-Created Stress. If we create fear and worry during the day, we have dreams involving fear and worry. Dreams are images the brain strings together, often in an attempt to resolve the stress we created while we were awake during the day. Dreaming is a little like watching an internal movie while we're sleeping.

Dreams are not observable FACTS that you observe with your senses (i.e., an elephant in your dream isn't an ACTUAL elephant—it's just an image).

What most of us don't realize is that our brains are creating illusions both day and night; our daytime thoughts are also illusions. These illusions are not FACTS observable by our senses. And if we believe and respond to them as if they ARE, we move them into the fantasy arena. We're not talking here about visualizing dreams, goals, or events you want to actualize in your life—that is an active, creative process. We are talking about the rote, mechanical reactions that our brains regurgitate out of habit.

When we accept and respond to our daytime illusions as REAL/FACT, that IS stress and creates a contradiction in the brain.

Example:

Let's say you have dinner plans with your friend, Jim, to meet at a restaurant. You're in an important work meeting that's running over its scheduled time, and your cell phone is on low battery. You don't want to leave the meeting, and you can't text Jim. For a half-hour until the meeting is finished you react with Self-Created Stress statements, *Jim's going to be upset! I have to call Jim ASAP!*

Yet you are not telling Jim anything HERE. The brain again is caught in a contradiction.

Indirectly you are telling the brain: THE BODY/MOUTH/I SHOULD BE CALLING Jim. But Jim is not present HERE. The brain sees this contradiction. It's supposed to tell Jim that you're going to be late, but it's not doing that HERE. That very contradiction is worry and stress.

The separation between what is actually going on, and what you want the brain or body to do, is stress. It causes the brain to go into panic mode, resulting in an adrenaline rush, or a tightened stomach, etc.

When you see you've run low on food, you know food is at the store, and you go when you can. When you realize the change in dinner plans, you know you have to call Jim, and you call him when you are able to. These are normal responses. But overreactions that heighten stress are also illusions that contradict our senses.

Sometimes you might rehearse a conversation in your head to work out what you want to say to someone. Instead of dividing your attention between HERE and that conversation, try to wait until you actually see the person to have a real conversation with them. Your intelligence HERE will be active and know what to say. Trust it.

You might ask, *Are you asking me to get rid of all my thoughts?*

No. But don't accept that the brain needs stress and illusions to function with intelligence. MIND is the brain operating with intelligence, awareness, and intuition. In the morning you don't need to think, *I need to put on my socks now!* You KNOW what to do, and do it, without making it a stressful action filled with illusion and contradiction. You get up, see your bare feet, and pull on a pair of socks.

This is thought *in action*. You don't tell yourself, *I have to put on my socks ASAP!* With the implied, *Or something bad will happen!*

You might be thinking, *Wait a minute! Many things I do in relationships, or at work, are way more complicated than pulling on a pair of socks!*

That is true. However, if you operate HERE, things are broken down to ONE action at a time, allowing that action to be performed efficiently and without creating stress, no matter how complicated it is.

~

Every Challenge Has Hidden Positives—Find Them

Research shows that the highest performing business teams are those that receive five to six positive statements from supervisors for every one negative comment. This means that to perform at our best we need to mostly think and speak positively about ourselves and our lives.

I was a master of finding fault with situations. *I won't enjoy the dinner party. What I'm hoping for won't happen. I don't have enough experience to get that job. That's nice, but…*I thought it was critical thinking, but it was a negative Self-Created Stress habit that increased my anxiety and argumentativeness. Worry created the habit, and the statements I told myself created illusions that I embraced as FACT.

A negative Self-Created Stress focus does not make us happy and takes more energy than it gives. It also brings us into conflict, inside and outside, with what we are reacting to, further draining our energy.

Any activity that takes more emotional energy from us than it gives is not worth hanging on to.

A rainy day might allow time to cook a meal or do a chore you previously haven't had time to do. Frigid cold days are great for a writer.

You can't see the positives in any situation if you are looking for the negatives.

This can also apply to social situations. If we decide the server isn't bringing us our food fast enough, we may complain. That's energy and work that we have created for ourselves.

Complaints affect servers' jobs and lives and create stress for ourselves and others.

I once gave a card to a friend showing a burnt building in the foreground, with the bright moon shining in the night sky in the background. On the card were the words: *Barn burned down, now I can see the moon.*

We are often thrown challenges that do not feel *perfect*. What makes everything in life perfect, including ourselves, is the ability to accept things without reacting with negative Self-Created Stress thoughts, words, or actions. This leaves us free to be peaceful and experience beauty and joy. Acceptance allows us the freedom to act, instead of react.

When the barn burns down, look for the shining moon.

TRY THIS

1) Each day, say or think one positive, repetitive phrase. It should counter a strong negative reaction in your life. Work at it. Write it down. Tape it to a mirror. Whatever time you've spent reinforcing negative Self-Created Stress patterns, it's worth putting equal effort into something inspiring. Smile as you say it. Do this for thirty days.

PAUSE HERE TO THINK OF A POSITIVE PHRASE FOR YOURSELF.

Anytime you find yourself making negative statements, rephrase them into a positive one. If you don't catch yourself until later, that's okay, and it's still worth doing. The brain will note any changes you are intending. Intent matters! It's not a wasted effort!

Examples:

Replace: *Everything is going downhill in the world!* with *Nature is beautiful.*

Replace: *I don't think things will work out!* with *Everything always works out for the best!* or *I will find a positive in whatever happens!*

PAUSE HERE TO REPHRASE NEGATIVE STATEMENTS YOU SOMETIMES MAKE.

2) Play with situations that irritate you:
   - I had to park so far away! *So I got a nice walk in.*
   - The bus was late! *So I meditated.*
   - Someone blasted their music! *So I hummed to it.*

3) All of these situations can be interrupted by using playful exaggeration.
   - *Everything is going downhill in the world!* can change to *The doughnut is rolling into a field of mud. Bloop! Bloop!*
   - *I don't think things will work out!* can change to *Gorilla is going to lose all his hair again!*
   - *I had to park so far away!* can change to *My feet are going to sing lullabies to me tonight!*

Again: interrupt, use humor in playful exaggerations, logic isn't important, and smile.

PAUSE HERE TO WRITE DOWN THREE NEGATIVE THOUGHTS YOU BRING TO SITUATIONS OR ACTIVITIES, A POSITIVE DETAIL, AND A PLAYFUL EXAGGERATION.

A) Negative/Critical Thought:

_____

B) Positive Detail:

_____

C) Playful Exaggeration:

_____

Say, think, & visualize the playful exaggeration, and smile!

A) Negative/Critical Thought:

_____

B) Positive Detail:

_____

C) Playful Exaggeration:

_____

Say, think, & visualize the playful exaggeration, and smile!

A) Negative/Critical Thought:

_____

B) Positive Detail:

_____

C) Playful Exaggeration:

_____

Say, think, & visualize the playful exaggeration, and smile!

PRACTICE

1) **Scripting**

Write a small journal entry daily *as if you have already succeeded and are living the life of your dreams.* Be as specific as you can. You can focus on one area or your whole life. Visualize the specifics of your dream.

Do this daily for one month. It will force you to view your situation positively, and program your brain and mind to seek these results. I thank Linda West for teaching me this.

Example:

Here is a scripting example from a friend in real estate:

Taking three weeks off because I can. I have money in the bank and clients are all squared away until after the first of the year. It's time to recharge after a fabulous year of change. I am going to visit a friend in Vietnam with my wife and daughter.

We will spend a week at the beach and tour the country with my friend as our guide. This should be an awesome trip. I closed on thirty transactions this year. Fifteen of them I partnered with a newer agent, and let them do the footwork and heavy lifting. They win, I win. How sweet it is.

PAUSE HERE TO PRACTICE SCRIPTING NOW.

Your script can be as short or long as you want to make it. Visualize your script as if you are there HERE. Smile and have fun!

~

The more you focus on positives, or those you want to draw into your life, the less room there will be for negative Self-Created Stress reactions. The brain will follow whatever path you set for it.

CHAPTER 10

Letting Go of Conflict, Rumors, & Opinions

*Everyone has a fresh chance daily to be
a new person if we allow it.*

People often hold onto past conflicts, hurts, or grudges. If someone insulted you, and every time you see them you remember that insult as if it were new, maybe you don't say, *Hello.*

When you allow memories to be the only thing that determines your current reactions to people, you are living in the illusion of the past, in Self-Created Stress. You are rejecting HERE, along with the person. You are also re-inflicting that previous hurt or pain on yourself.

Worse, you won't be able to see if the person has changed, or if your perception was based on one moment in a bad day. You are now a prisoner to those memories, illusions, and past events—captured in your neural net—which lead to creating limiting thoughts that control your behavior, actions, and words.

Yet wherever you are, everything and everyone is new.

Remember, negative emotions you carry around hurt you the most. They increase your underlying stress, which harms you physically.

Are you carrying any conflicts, large or small, forward? Any grudges? Are you repeating stories of hurt or displeasure to family, friends, or coworkers?

Begin a new life, HERE, and approach each person and action as an opportunity to learn, change, be positive, and share love.

TRY THIS

1) Notice if you carry around a hurt, conflict, or grudge, and are repeating it to others or yourself over and over. Next time, instead of repeating it, take a deep breath and let it go. See if you can say something positive about the person instead.

2) Find an empty room and loudly complain. Playfully exaggerate how a person or business is ruining your life so your happiness can never recover. Examples of playful exaggeration are, *Bill is ruining my clothing! Stacey is making my makeup run! George is conjuring a rain cloud over my head!*

   And then force laughter at everything bothering you. This doesn't minimize your situation, but it does put it into proper context.

PAUSE HERE TO PLAYFULLY EXAGGERATE AN ARGUMENT WITH SOMEONE YOU ARE STILL UPSET WITH AND HANGING ONTO A HURT, GRUDGE, OR CONFLICT.

3) Laugh. Laughter yoga is practiced in 100 countries. The doctor in India who founded the concept wanted a way to get people to laugh routinely. Research shows that practicing laughter has the same beneficial effect as laughing spontaneously.[12]

Laughter helps create positive brain chemistry, releases stress, energizes the emotions, and calms the body. It is an instant window into a meditative state as well as good exercise. Cultures with great health and longevity are ones that laugh daily and often.

PRACTICE

A) Write or think about someone in your life you still hold a grudge against, felt hurt by, or have an ongoing inner conflict with.

B) Next write down what was done to you.

C) Find one good thing about the person, employer, or business. This will help you move on and leave the negative patterns behind.

D) Lastly create one playful exaggeration about the hurt or grudge.

Example 1:

A) Name: *George, a casual friend*

B) Hurt or Grudge: *He always interrupts me*

C) One Positive: *He offers great advice*

D) Playful Exaggeration: *If he interrupts me again, I'll shrink to the size of a mouse!*

Example 2:

A) Name: *Car mechanic*

B) Hurt or Grudge: *He took too long to fix my car!*

C) One Positive: *My car runs well*

D) Playful Exaggeration: *I waited so long my hair turned white!*

Example 3:

A) Name: *Jason, a brother*

B) Hurt or Grudge: *He is often critical of me*

C) One Positive: *He loves his family*

D) Playful Exaggeration: *The next time he criticizes me, I'll turn into a pile of dust!*

PAUSE HERE TO CONSIDER ANYONE YOU HAVE ONGOING NEGATIVE REACTIONS TO, WHAT CAUSED THE HURT OR GRUDGE, AND ONE POSITIVE ABOUT THE PERSON. CREATE A PLAYFUL EXAGGERATION.

A) Name:

_____

B) Hurt/Grudge:

_____

C) One Positive:

_____

D) Playful Exaggeration:

_____

Say, think, & visualize the playful exaggeration, and smile!

A) Name:

_____

B) Hurt/Grudge:

_____

C) One Positive:

_____

D) Playful Exaggeration:

_____

Say, think, & visualize the playful exaggeration, and smile!

A) Name:

_____

B) Hurt/Grudge:

_____

C) One Positive:

_____

D) Playful Exaggeration:

_____

Say, think, & visualize the playful exaggeration, and smile!

This exercise is another way to focus on the positive with everyone you meet and end the habitual hurt reactions and illusions you are still carrying around.

~

LET RUMORS AND OPINIONS GO

Rumors & Opinions are not facts and distort reality.

Let's say there's a rumor at work that there might be layoffs. Your reaction is, *Oh no, I could lose my job!* Beneath that reaction are the Self-Created Stress words, *What will I do? What if I can't find another job? I will lose my house! I won't be able to pay rent! I hope it's not me!*

All this reactivity is caused by a rumor that may or may not be true. All day you think about it and are on edge. In essence you are reacting to an illusion of possible danger or harm to yourself.

That night, while trying to sleep, your brain won't let it go. You keep thinking, worrying, and creating stress. You don't sleep well. Yet HERE you are not laid off. You are safe in bed and no one is attacking you. Your fearful thoughts and reactivity do NOT match the factual situation of HERE.

Later you find out the rumor was false, or maybe layoffs are a year away, or are coming in days. In all of these scenarios, the worry, sleeplessness, and reactivity do not make your job more secure or help find a solution if you lose your job.

The fearful reaction feels *life or death*. The brain is in survival mode: *I'm at risk of losing everything and ending up on the street! No housing! No food! I could die!* These are all illusions, and not FACTS HERE.

If you lose your job, it may bring serious financial loss and hardship requiring problem-solving or seeking help. Why compound the reality with emotional reactions that stress you, wear you out, and adversely affect those around you?

Fear and anger often are overreactions that don't fit the facts; we react to our created inner world of thoughts, images, and illusions instead of responding to what is factual and observable around us HERE.

I once misread information and thought I was going to have to pay $1500 for marketing help. I couldn't sleep, so I made up playful exaggerations such as, *Gorilla wasted 1500 bananas!* The playful exaggerations ended my obsessive thoughts and worry. And later I found out I had to pay $50, not $1500.

Stay with the facts of any situation, and HERE, and it will be easier to remain calm through any storm.

TRY THIS

1) In any Self-Created Stress situation, when you find yourself fictionalizing to the point where it feels *life or death*, your stomach is tight, your shoulders bunched, your skin sweaty, your jaw clenched, or your thoughts racing, ask yourself these questions:
   - ○ *Is a tiger charging me right now, ready to eat me?*
     Yes   No
   - ○ *Am I in mortal danger?*   **Yes   No**
   - ○ *Could I die now?*   **Yes   No**

If the answer to any of these questions is *Yes*, then RUN! If not, these questions are another way to put your fear, concern, or worry into proper context in your life. Let your overreaction go and remain calm and objective. This is a fun exercise, useful in any Self-Created Stress situation you find yourself in.

2) A) Another question to ask yourself any time you feel stress or any negative emotion is this: *Am I safe HERE?*

   Pay attention to your body, not your thoughts. *Is your body warm enough? Do you have enough food? Are you safe from physical harm?* Note the difference between the observations about your body and the reactions to your stress-driven thoughts.

   B) When you are NOT stressed or worried, sit in a chair and notice the calm, peaceful quality of your body.

Create playful exaggerations that you are in danger. E.g., *I'm falling off a waterfall! A rhino is charging me! I'm jumping out of an airplane with no parachute!*

This may seem silly, but it allows you to see that the thoughts are NOT real and NOT actual danger. Yet your reaction to them can be harmful if you believe thoughts and images in your brain are the REAL/FACTUAL thing that they merely represent.

C) Another way to put your problems into perspective is to ask yourself, *On my deathbed, will this be remembered as important? What about next week?*

PRACTICE

A) Write down or reflect on the most recent situations you distorted in your mind with Self-Created Stress statements.

B) Next list the verifiable FACTS of the situation.

C) List one positive statement about the actual result.

D) Create a playful exaggeration.

Example 1:

A) Self-Created Stress statements: You get out of bed fifteen minutes late and think: *I screwed up and will be late for work! I'll be in trouble!* Perhaps you imagine a drama scene of your supervisor yelling at you in front of coworkers.

B) Verifiable Facts: *I will be fifteen minutes late.*

C) A Positive Result: *I was late, but my boss didn't say anything.*

D) Playful Exaggeration: *My boss is going to tie me to a chair and spin me in circles!*

Or create something equally silly or exaggerated to end your own Self-Created Stress response.

Example 2:

A) Self-Created Stress statements: You forgot your dental appointment and think: *Oh no! I forgot my dental appointment. They'll be angry!* Perhaps you imagine your dentist refusing future appointments.

B) Verifiable Facts: *I forgot the dental appointment. I have to call them.*

C) A Positive Result: *The dental office was fine with rescheduling my appointment, since an emergency filled their schedule.*

D) Playful Exaggeration: *My dentist is going to banish me to a small island in the South Pacific!* (Which you might actually enjoy.)

Sometimes there is no positive result. Your supervisor might give you a warning or fire you. This still is not *life or death*, or worthy of creating stress for your body and mind. Remaining calm in any situation doesn't guarantee a good result, but it guarantees the best result. Remaining calm is always best for your body, brain, mind, and life.

PAUSE HERE TO THINK OF THREE DISTORTED RESPONSES YOU CREATED. REPHRASE THEM WITH THE VERIFIABLE FACTS. LIST ONE POSITIVE RESULT, AND CREATE A PLAYFUL EXAGGERATION.

A) Self-Created Stress Statement that Distorted a Situation:

_____

B) Verifiable Facts:

_____

C) A Positive Result:

_____

D) Playful Exaggeration:

_____

Say, think, & visualize the playful exaggeration, and smile!

A) Self-Created Stress Statement that Distorted a Situation:

_____

B) Verifiable Facts:

_____

C) A Positive Result:

_____

D) Playful Exaggeration:

_____

Say, think, & visualize the playful exaggeration, and smile!

A) Self-Created Stress Statement that Distorted a Situation:

_____

B) Verifiable Facts:

_____

C) A Positive Result:

_____

D) Playful Exaggeration:

_____

Say, think, & visualize the playful exaggeration, and smile!

This exercise helps you see how much you distort situations and will help you develop objectivity and remain with the facts. This prevents Self-Created Stress reactions from taking over your mind and emotions. Opinions are distortions and illusions, not facts. Any distortion leads to stress at some level through arguments, internal or external conflict, and negative emotions. Being objective makes it easier to remain calm.

~

Note: One of the disturbing patterns of the last decades is that opinions have been presented as important as scientific facts. An opinion is not a fact, not a theory, nor a hypothesis based on observable events. It's just what you feel like believing. An illusion.

Politicians and the news media often focus on opinions, not facts, wasting energy and continuing division and tribalism. They reinforce opinions to advance personal and corporate agendas to get votes or sell ads and products.

Frequently these opinions are based on lies, distortions, exaggerations, or bias: all illusions. This adds more confusion and more distrust to society.

Example:

Many people who are not scientists don't believe human activity is causing global warming/climate change. They think their belief is as valid as the overwhelming scientific research showing that human activity is largely responsible for climate change.

Why do people discount science in favor of opinions?

In the last decades, corporations and politicians created disinformation campaigns using disreputable scientists. They also denied the factual dangers associated with tobacco, global warming, GMOs (genetically modified organisms/food), pesticides, and even Covid-19, dismissing facts as opinions. They wanted the public to believe, for example, that global warming was a matter of opinion, and that your opinion is just as strong an argument as facts from scientific research. The motive to support lies or opinions over facts is often profit or power.

In 1633 the Catholic Church believed Earth was the center of the universe. When Galileo discovered that the sun was the center of our solar system, the Church told him to recant or be tortured; he recanted. The Church then confined Galileo to lifelong house arrest.

It took the Church 359 years, until 1992, to admit Galileo was right. Yet the facts were always facts, despite what the Church believed. Opinions don't change facts.

Smart phones, computers, cars, planes, shoes, clothing, appliances, DVDs, TVs, etc., are all designed and produced using technology based on science.

Why reject the same scientific method that is the basis for creating all of our goods, when it is applied to global warming, ocean acidification, agricultural problems related to commercial farming, and destruction of ecosystems worldwide?

A majority of scientists arriving at the same conclusions through fact-based research is not an opinion. Decision-making based on opinions puts all of us at risk for severe weather, cancer, food shortages, pandemics, and many other consequences.

When you look at life, honor facts, not opinions.

Intelligence operating HERE never acts out of opinion, bias, or illusion, because our definition of intelligence is awareness operating HERE; living based on observable facts.

CHAPTER 11

Love, Kindness, & Loneliness

What matters above all else? Love.

To love others, we must love ourselves. Love requires clarity and the absence of conflict, stress, illusions, and divided awareness.

A famous Buddhist monk who traveled the world told me that people in the United States are more self-critical than people in any country he visited. This is another form of Self-Created Stress.

We learned from the saber-toothed tiger example that our brains are wired to focus on negatives more than positives. We remember a criticism or mistake for a long time, but a compliment might quickly fade away. In the distant past, focusing on *bad things or threats* helped individuals survive. Now this pattern more often creates unhappiness, conflict, and stress.

The possibilities for self-criticism with Self-Created Stress are endlessly hurtful; *I'm stupid. I'm not good. I'm a failure. I don't do anything right. I don't look very nice.* These are opinions, not FACTS. Illusions.

If we don't love ourselves, we won't be happy and free to find our passions, which limits our joy. If we are unhappy, it is hard to interact with others in a loving manner.

It is also self-critical to compare yourself to someone else: *They look better. They're smarter. They have all the luck. They're prettier. They dress better.* In effect you're saying to yourself, *I'm not as attractive, I'm not as smart, I have worse luck, I don't dress as nicely.*

Western society loves to compare everyone, and our culture tends to label everyone as a success or failure. *He's #1, the best, the leader! She's just a #6, just so-so. John got a C; Carlos got an A!* etc. Comparison is a destructive, negative process.

We all learn differently, and have different abilities, potentials, and characteristics to offer.

Another irony is that when we criticize others, it may feel as if we are protecting or just expressing ourselves. In reality we are draining our energy and hurting our chances to be loving or kind.

Self-Created Stress occurs in reactions to individuals or groups. We can criticize or dislike a whole country of people, a race, a religious group, a skin color, a political group, or any group.

Criticism of others creates division and internal and external conflict. This Self-Created Stress separates and isolates us from people, weakening our relationships.

If we criticize others, we most likely also criticize ourselves. Criticism limits our empathy and awareness for others. We all have equal value, deserve love, and deserve to love ourselves fully.

To be truly happy, become your own greatest fan. I often tell students: *Imagine the most loving parent or the greatest cheerleader in the world, and think about what they would say to a child to comfort and encourage them. Then be that loving parent and cheerleader for yourself with positive messages.*

To spread love everywhere, share those same uplifting positive messages with everyone. You will create a loving world for yourself that can't be taken away.

TRY THIS

1) Whenever you notice you are criticizing yourself, interrupt the process and replace it with a cheerleading/loving parent comment to yourself. Work at this. Your whole identity can change to a more loving, positive personality.

2) Each day find one unique positive thing you do and praise yourself for it. Tell others or give yourself a pat on the back. Celebrate your actions! It can be the simplest of things: *I got up on time. I held a door open for someone. I exercised. I gave someone a compliment. I did my best on a test. I listened to a bird sing.*

   Every time I complete a writing task, I often say, *Good job, Geoff!* or *Fantastic job, Geoff!* or *Awesome, Geoff!* I mean it, enjoy it, and it brings a smile to my face.

PAUSE HERE AND PRACTICE GIVING YOURSELF POSITIVE PRAISE.

3) When I hear myself criticizing someone, I've found it helpful to remind myself that:
   ○ *Everyone is part of my family.*
   ○ *Everyone has good qualities and I will find them.*
   ○ *Everyone wants to be happy and loved.*

PAUSE HERE AND PRACTICE THIS NOW.

4) If you find that you are criticizing yourself over a "mistake" you made, or something you regret having said (apologizing is the best solution here), use playful exaggerations to put it into perspective:

This mistake will turn my face blue! I will turn into a toad!
They will replay my criticism in the international news
in 67 languages!

We all learn from stumbling. The word *mistake* only exists in our heads. It doesn't exist unless we attach it to an action, event, or something we said. Congratulate yourself on seeing where you would like to improve and move on. Do your best, which is good enough.

PRACTICE

1) A) Consider critical, negative, or limiting thoughts you have about yourself.

    B) Create a Positive Cheerleader Statement.

    C) Create a playful exaggeration of your self-criticism.

Example 1:

A) Self-Criticism: *I always make mistakes.*

B) Positive Cheerleader Statement: *I love myself, no matter what I do.*

C) Playful Exaggeration: *I've been voted the Galaxy's King of Mistakes!*

Example 2:

A) Self-Criticism: *I don't look very good.*

B) Positive Cheerleader Statement: *I'm wonderful and lovable!*

C) Playful Exaggeration: *I've cracked every mirror I've ever looked at, even a mile away!*

PAUSE HERE TO CONSIDER THREE SELF-CRITICISMS, EVEN AT A SUBTLE LEVEL. CREATE A POSITIVE CHEER-

LEADER STATEMENT TO REPLACE EACH CRITICISM. CREATE A PLAYFUL EXAGGERATION.

A) Self-Criticism:

_____

B) Positive Cheerleader Statement:

_____

C) Playful Exaggeration:

_____

Say, think, & visualize the playful exaggeration, and smile!

A) Self-Criticism:

_____

B) Positive Cheerleader Statement:

_____

C) Playful Exaggeration:

_____

Say, think, & visualize the playful exaggeration, and smile!

A) Self-Criticism:

_____

B) Positive Cheerleader Statement:

_____

C) Playful Exaggeration:

_____

Say, think, & visualize the playful exaggeration, and smile!

2) Look in the mirror and say, *I forgive you,* _____. Fill in the blank with the name of someone you criticize, hold a grudge against, or are in conflict with.

This is another way to end your own inner conflict and stress, which will move you toward harmony with everyone.

PAUSE TO PRACTICE THIS MIRROR WORK NOW.

3) Consider a criticism you think or say about others.

A) Write or consider the names of people you find irritating, dislike, or criticize.

B) Write down what you dislike about them.

C) Write one positive thing about them. Finding at least one positive attribute about someone is important. List more than one if you can. If this is difficult, it indicates how much you focus on negatives.

D) Write a playful exaggeration about the trait you dislike.

Example 1:

A) Name: *Barry, who is an acquaintance*

B) Criticism: *Barry is always late to choir practice*

C) Positives: *Barry is a great singer, takes voice criticism well, brings coffee for everyone*

D) Playful Exaggeration: *Barry is so late we have spiderwebs on our clothing by the time he arrives!*

Example 2:

A) Name: *Alyssa, my sister*

B) Criticism: *Alyssa is a know-it-all*

C) Positives: *Alyssa cares about her children and husband, has a sense of humor*

D) Playful Exaggeration: *Alyssa knows everything, so I can forget about Google and just ask her!*

PAUSE HERE TO WRITE DOWN THE NAME OF ANYONE YOU CRITICIZE. NEXT WRITE DOWN THE CRITICISM. FIND ONE OR MORE POSITIVES ABOUT THE PERSON. LASTLY CREATE A PLAYFUL EXAGGERATION.

A) Name:

_____

B) Criticism:

_____

C) Positives:

_____

D) Playful Exaggeration:

_____

Say, think, & visualize the playful exaggeration, and smile!

A) Name:

_____

B) Criticism:

_____

C) Positives:

_____

D) Playful Exaggeration:

_____

Say, think, & visualize the playful exaggeration, and smile!

A) Name:

_____

B) Criticism:

_____

C) Positives:

_____

D) Playful Exaggeration:

_____

Say, think, & visualize the playful exaggeration, and smile!

~

This exercise can change your viewpoint and your relationship with everyone.

KINDNESS

Be heroic every day.

One student I worked with often arrived at school angry. A number of people responded to him with their own Self-Created Stress tape of, *What an idiot! How dare he talk to me like that! I'm a staff member and he's just a student!* Others either ignored him or were verbally combative with him. This increased his conflict, anger, and internal stress.

Responding to someone's anger in kind means you're doing the same thing, reacting with rote Self-Created Stress responses.

I always said hello to the student and smiled, regardless of his running Self-Created Stress tape of, *I hate school! Everyone is stupid here! I don't want to be here!*—which resulted in his anger.

As you increase your awareness of Self-Created Stress, you see others playing their own Self-Created Stress tapes. This can help you be empathetic to everyone.

I never took the student's anger personally. I observed that he was suffering and I wanted to help, which made it easy to smile and give a friendly greeting.

At his graduation ceremony speech, the student said he would never forget the staff member who always greeted him with a smile, despite his frequent bad moods.

Whether you want to or not, for better or for worse, you influence everyone around you. If you take this responsibility seriously, you will try to be a positive influence in every life you touch. That is heroic.

If you help ease the stress of others (vs. reacting negatively), you then are not strengthening your rote neural pathways and you are not strengthening their Self-Created Stress responses.

One sign of excellence is how someone handles life and their relationships when faced with challenges. It is far easier to be carefree when everything is going great than when faced with adversity.

TRY THIS

1) When someone is harsh or unkind, they are playing out their own illusions and Self-Created Stress tapes. How

can you avoid reacting with your own Self-Created Stress tape?

A)   You can leave the situation, ask a question, respond with kindness, or just listen quietly. You can smile even if they don't respond, although sometimes a smile will just trigger anger.

B)   If someone says something unkind to you, playfully exaggerate it shortly after with something like, *It's the end of my career as I know it! This comment will go viral on YouTube!* And smile!

Once you practice this, you will be surprised how easy it can be to end your reactions to others. This doesn't mean you allow verbal abuse; speak up if you need to. But don't react and dwell on it.

2)   Smile at everyone you contact in the service industry and ask how their day is going. Smiles are contagious![13]

Ask them what they are doing to enjoy the day or season. Be personal. Include them in your family.

PRACTICE

1)   List three cashiers, attendants, or service people you interact with. Record one positive question you asked them, and their response.

Example:

A)   Who did you meet? *Hair stylist*

B)   Question asked: *I asked how her summer is going*

C)   Her response: *She loves to plant flowers, enjoys her grandkids, and seemed happy to share that*

PAUSE AND WRITE DOWN THREE CLERKS, CUSTOMER SERVICE REPS, POSTMAN, ETC. THAT YOU MEET, A QUESTION YOU WILL ASK THEM, AND THEIR RESPONSE.

A) Who did you meet?

_____

B) Question asked?

_____

C) Their response?

_____

A) Who did you meet?

_____

B) Question asked?

_____

C) Their response?

_____

A) Who did you meet?

_____

B) Question asked?

_____

C) Their response?

_____

If you include everyone in your "family," it makes your world a friendly, warm home, instead of a place filled with strangers and rote and rehearsed interactions. Harmony vs. conflict. Calm vs. stress. Master vs. Servant.

~

Note: People are wired to be social and empathetic toward each other; our brains have mirror neurons.[14] We all send body language signals about our feelings, and the mirror neurons allow us to pick up emotions from each other. Therefore smiling and kindness are important for everyone! Conversely, if a friend or someone is depressed or down, you might feel your own emotional spirit sinking too—that response may be your mirror neurons picking up their emotions. Thus always make sure to ask yourself when around others, *What is their emotion? What is mine?*

~

LONELINESS

Alone is not lonely.

Covid-19 has intensified isolation and loneliness for some people. However, feeling lonely was common even before Covid-19.

People walking down a crowded sidewalk can feel as lonely as someone living alone in an apartment. However there is a real component to the urge to be with others because humans are wired to be social, to have contact and touch. Some people feel this less strongly than others, often due to genetics, and they are content to spend the majority of their time alone. But some of us feel a strong urge to be social. With Covid-19, you might feel even more isolated—and thus lonely—than others due to social restrictions.

The feeling of loneliness is another negative emotional reaction to the thought or observation, *I'm alone.* Examples of negative reactions to this might be; *No one loves me! I have no friends!* Sometimes this can also lead to despair and hopelessness.

Negative reactions (which you might not even be aware of) to the thought, *I am alone*, might also include; *My life is a failure! My life has no meaning! I feel empty!* Beneath these reactions might also be an implied, *My life is sad! I can't go on! My happiness is destroyed! What's the point of living?*

Playful exaggerations can short-circuit any feelings of loneliness, sadness, or despair. The goal is to change the reactions to your thoughts—and that will change your thoughts. If you observe, *I am alone*, that observation does not have to result in feeling lonely. And, more importantly, on a planet of 7.8+ billion people, you most certainly are *not alone*.

TRY THIS

1) When you notice any feelings of loneliness, sadness, or despair—remember—these are reactions to thoughts! They are not facts. They are illusions. Don't accept them!

   Thus when you notice any negative thoughts or feelings related to *I am lonely*, play with them! Some examples of playful exaggerations are:

   ❍ *On a planet of 7.8+ billion people there is no man, woman, or child who will ever speak to me again!*

   ❍ *I'll have to go into deep space to find an alien to connect with!*

   ❍ *I will have to talk to my plants or pets more!*

Humor is a great antidote to any negative emotion. But it is even better to end the habit of reacting to your thoughts, and ending those thought patterns in your brain. None of this is to minimize your emotions, but you want to end the repetitive reactions (emotions) to your thoughts that cause you pain and misery.

PAUSE HERE TO PRACTICE EXAGGERATED STATEMENTS ABOUT LONELINESS.

2) On a practical level, if you want more social interaction, do computer or phone: Zoom meetings; Google hangouts; WhatsApp; or Skype. Join MeetUp groups. Connect with people that share your passions and interests. Talk to anyone you have contact with throughout the day. Phone or text friends and family if you are experiencing more isolation.

3) Change your story and outlook to observe the FACTS and your INTENTIONS. Do this by changing *I am lonely!* to *I am alone, but I'm able to talk to others, find connections, & end negative reactions to my thoughts.*

PAUSE HERE TO PRACTICE THIS NOW.

PRACTICE

1) Mirror Work

Self-love counteracts feelings of loneliness. The goal is to feel that love deeply, as a FACT. Practicing self-love is important in anyone's life.

The sentence, *I really love you,* is even more powerful when you look in a mirror and say it to yourself. Do this every time you see a mirror, and smile while doing it. Allow yourself to feel love for yourself. Feel the warmth of it in your heart and body. If you don't feel it, keep doing it anyway. Practice helps.

You can extend this to: *I love my body. I love my efforts. Good job! I forgive you (for whatever criticism you have of yourself).* Say whatever your inner child needs to hear to feel loved and cared for.

This practice, called mirror work by Louise Hay, can help you turn around how you feel about life and yourself in a very short time. You can even carry around a small mirror to repeat this as often as you feel is helpful. Perform mirror work daily.

PAUSE HERE TO PRACTICE LOOKING INTO A MIRROR AND MAKE LOVING STATEMENTS TO YOURSELF.

2) Do mirror work with statements such as: *I love my body. I will treat my body with respect, feed it healthy food, exercise it, and take care of it. I will meet my social needs so that I thrive in my life!*

PAUSE HERE TO PRACTICE MIRROR WORK NOW.

~

Self-love, love for others, and kindness will help you engage lovingly with everyone in your life, no matter how many people are in it. And playful exaggerations will interrupt and eventually erase loneliness reactions to the factual statement, *I am alone.* What you will discover instead is that joy, creativity, and intelligence will blossom!

CHAPTER 12

Healthy Brain & Nature, Body Intelligence, & Real-World Stressful Problems

If we are trying to rewire our brain, obviously we want to keep it healthy!

Decades of modern research shows that to optimize the brain health of children and adults, the following five things are essential:

1) A healthy diet
2) Spending time in nature
3) Exercising
4) Minimizing screen time (phones, computers, TVs, video games, etc.)
5) Good sleep

HEALTHY DIET

Let's examine diet first, which is a struggle for many. A healthy diet can be simplified to a few sentences: Eat whole, unprocessed foods without additives or sugar. As often as possible, eat organic food to minimize chemicals and GMOs in the body. Whole vegetables and fruits are loaded with antioxidants that research shows are necessary for a healthy brain.[15]

The body—guided by mind—has great intelligence. If you listen, it will tell you not only how much to eat, but what to eat.

My healthy father, who is ninety-three as of this writing, has never liked broccoli and avoids eating it. Broccoli is considered a healthy food, packed with vitamins, minerals, and antioxidants. But it tastes horrible to him. This is his body's way of saying, *Don't eat this food. It's not good for you!*

Everyone has a different genetic makeup. The idea that one particular diet, fast, type of juicing, or food is great for everyone is nonsense. Discover what your body wants to keep you healthy. With practice and focus, you can access your body intelligence when you are shopping for food, out for dinner, or in your own kitchen.

Every time you see food ask, *What would be best for me to eat?* Let your body answer, not your thoughts. Do you feel an impulse while shopping to buy some Brussels sprouts or a particular type of fruit?

For dinner, do you sense the need to eat a small meal, a vegetarian meal, or a meat dish? Pay attention to these subtle signals. In time they will be stronger and easier to recognize. As you end illusions in your life, your body's signals HERE will feel stronger and this process will be easier to identify.

~

Note 1: If you are heavily addicted to a diet of sugar, fat, salt, and processed foods, it is extremely hard for the body intelligence to operate. Your addictions dominate what you want to taste and eat. If you move to a healthier diet, the body's messages will become easier to understand and follow. When you rid yourself of any addiction (e.g., to junk food), your intuition regarding all aspects of well-being improves.

~

Note 2: Another way to use visualization to your benefit is for your health. Jay, a close friend of mine, was paralyzed with polio at age twelve. Doctors told him he would never walk again. Jay's new-age mother said to him, *Ignore the doctors. Tell your body to heal the nerves running down your spine, arms, and legs.* Jay visualized this, and ended up playing basketball and doing anything else he wanted to do. Direct the body to heal. You have nothing to lose. This doesn't mean you ignore doctors or don't seek medical or alternative healthcare help. But it does mean you enlist another creative aspect of your being to help yourself heal.

~

SELF-CREATED STRESS CAN ISOLATE US FROM NATURE

Nature offers endless beauty if we see it clearly.

You may ask, *Why are we talking about nature in a book about stress?* Conflict in any area of our lives creates stress. Harming our planet is a form of conflict, and thus stress.

Also it is well-documented that nature calms, quiets, and destresses the brain.[16] Too many children are not connected to nature in their daily lives. And children who do spend time in nature naturally exercise more and spend less time on screens.

At the annual 2015 White House Easter Egg Roll, President Obama read Maurice Sendak's *Where the Wild Things Are* to a group of children outside. As Mr. Obama read a book about monsters, a honeybee buzzed around the children; they began to scream. Although the president tried to calm the children, they were slow to respond.

Children living on farms don't scream at bees. They see them as essential pollinators for many crops, and as honey producers.

Bees are hard workers, and without them our food chain would collapse.

If children hear adults discuss weather, nature, insects, and wild animals as adversaries, they learn to regard elements of nature with displeasure. *Bees might sting me! I could be in great pain! Sharks are dangerous! The humidity is horrible!*

Children living in cities often don't experience enough nature. They also don't hear about the importance of our ecosystems and the necessity of interacting with nature for our own health of mind, body, and spirit.

Self-Created Stress reactions to nature are another source of illusions resulting in worry, fear, and anxiety.

Example:

Many people express fear of sharks. Yet sharks eat sick fish, which keeps fish populations healthy so disease doesn't spread. This also protects the fish species we eat. Among over 400 species of sharks, only a dozen attack swimmers, with three species responsible for most attacks (great white, tiger, and bull). On average, six people die each year from shark attacks worldwide. Yet 100 million sharks are killed annually by people cutting off their fins for shark fin soup and throwing the shark back into the ocean to die.

The World Health Organization estimates that 1.25 million people die in car accidents worldwide yearly, while The National Highway Traffic Safety Administration (NHTSA) data shows 36,560 people were killed in car accidents in the U.S. in 2018. Cars pose a much greater lifetime danger to you than any animal ever will. Is anyone suggesting we kill all the deadly cars?

Mosquitoes spread disease and are a nuisance, but they also feed bats and birds. Male mosquitoes are pollinators. Likewise, you may react to rainy days with annoyance, but rain grows our food, fills our streams, rivers, lakes, and oceans, and nourishes our forests and wildlife. Rain is our lifeblood. It keeps everything alive and healthy.

Self-Created Stress can reduce parts of nature to an adversary, something we don't like. Saying, *I am unhappy about rain/bees/ sharks existing! I want it to change or end!* creates conflict within yourself, which is another form of stress. And you lose sight of the value and beauty of nature. Sharks, bees, and rain have great beauty, if you can see it.

If you focus on finding fault or detecting whatever displeases you in nature, you will not have the attention, focus, or awareness to see its beauty and positive impact on our lives or the lives of other creatures.

Nature is an integrated system where every part has value. Tribal people worldwide, now and in the past, valued and lived (and live) in harmony with nature. The rest of us can too.

TRY THIS

1) If you find yourself criticizing anything in nature, find out why that insect, wild animal, or plant has value to the ecosystem and value to people.

2) If you have a dislike or fear of a particular animal or insect, remind yourself of these things:

   ○ *The animal or insect has a valuable place in nature.*

   ○ *The animal or insect is not my sworn enemy. It is just trying to exist, like me.*

   ○ *This part of nature is not hurting me right now.*

For example, sharks are not a concern outside of the ocean. I love to swim, but I avoid ocean beaches because that's often where shark attacks occur. Sharks feed on injured fish in shallow water and mistake swimmers for sick fish, or surfers for seals. After tasting a person, sharks usually let them go. They don't like the way people taste!

PRACTICE

A) Write down insects, weather patterns, animals, or parts of nature that scare you, annoy you, that you dislike or even hate.

B) Write down why you dislike or hate them.

C) Write one positive detail about the animal, part of nature, or weather pattern. If you don't know a positive, research and find one.

D) Write down a playful exaggeration.

Example:

A) Nature Item Scared or Annoyed With: *sharks*

B) Why You Dislike It: *They are scary and sometimes bite people*

C) One Positive Detail: *Sharks are an amazing part of nature with spectacular strength and power, essential to keeping fish populations healthy*

D) Playful Exaggeration: *Sharks are chasing me down the street!*

PAUSE HERE TO LIST THREE ITEMS IN NATURE THAT YOU HAVE NEGATIVE REACTIONS TO, WHY YOU DISLIKE THEM, ONE POSITIVE DETAIL ABOUT EACH, & A PLAYFUL EXAGGERATION.

A) Nature Item Scared or Annoyed With:

_____

B) Why You Dislike It:

_____

C) One Positive Detail:

_____

D) Playful Exaggeration:

_____

Say, think, & visualize the playful exaggeration, and smile!

A) Nature Item Scared or Annoyed With:

_____

B) Why You Dislike It:

_____

C) One Positive Detail:

_____

D) Playful Exaggeration:

_____

Say, think, & visualize the playful exaggeration, and smile!

A) Nature Item Scared or Annoyed With:

_____

B) Why You Dislike It:

_____

C) One Positive Detail:

_____

D) Playful Exaggeration:

_____

Say, think, & visualize the playful exaggeration, and smile!

Conduct this exercise with children who display Self-Created Stress in reaction to any aspect of nature. Our planet has great beauty and doesn't charge an admission fee. It's our home and we are temporary guests. Help children understand the value and importance of nature, to see its beauty, and to safely enjoy it as often as possible. Make it a regular part of their lives.

~

EXERCISE, SCREEN TIME, & SLEEP

This is not a book about exercise or screen time. But there are some simple rules. Low impact exercises such as swimming, walking, biking, dancing, Qigong, and tai chi are excellent for the body at all ages. As people age they may need more weight-bearing exercises to keep up bone density. Find movements you love to do. I happen to love kung fu, swimming, and hiking. None of these forms of movement are 'exercise' to me; instead they are activities I never want to quit! Thus I never have to force myself to do them. Find something you love, that doesn't harm your body, and enjoy it!

Regarding screen time: Wear blue light blocking glasses whenever you are on computer or phone screens, especially from early evening on. The glasses protect your brain from blue light, which then doesn't interrupt your sleep. Get off all screens at least an hour before bedtime. Don't have wi-fi or lights of any kind on in your bedroom while sleeping.

In addition, go to bed the same time every night and finish eating at least 3+ hours before you go to bed. If you exercise, limit screen time, and reduce stress, sleep should improve! Good sleep is important for every area of your physical, mental, and emotional health, so make sure you focus on it!

Limit the time your children spend on screens, get them into nature, give them a healthy diet, and help them find exercise they love!

LISTENING TO YOUR BODY'S INTELLIGENCE HERE

It may feel difficult to keep all the components of a healthy life in harmony. Can you do this in a way that is easy, fluid, and requires little energy?

Yes.

It is a further extension of listening to your body's intelligence on what to eat.

Follow the action of your body (vs. thoughts), and it will always guide you with intelligence HERE. This means paying attention to what your body wants to do, eat, where to go, to get up, sit down, move, act, not act, etc. The body is guided by MIND.

If you practice this awareness, you never have to think about the next best course of action. The body is grounded HERE, with intelligence and mind. It will a provide action in harmony with your goals and dreams. Make it your intent to follow the body-mind connection. The days of *thinking your actions through* will transform into acting out of intelligence and awareness.

When you follow the action of the body instead of chasing thoughts, it is the combined intelligence/awareness of the mind, body, and brain that will guide you in harmony with HERE.

To learn how to do this, pay attention to what the body "wants to do," not what "thought wants the body to do"—e.g., eat a bag of chips, force exercise, avoid exercise, etc.

Acting out of thought eventually leads to discouragement, inaction, or giving up on things like a healthy diet and exercise plan. Following the action of the body is a little like intuition, but physically based in action, not thought.

Example:

After doing Qigong three hours a day for three months, my 'body intelligence' = mind + body + brain once guided me through seven hours of movements while I lay on my back on the floor. The energy 'pulled' me down to the floor. These types of automatic movements are more commonly witnessed in China, when people experience strong energy in the body as a result of practicing Qigong.

The movements were unknown to me, but the results were that my shoulders, over an inch off the floor at the beginning, lay flat on the floor at the end. This is one of many examples of the body intelligence directing activity it 'knows' is for your best interest.

Another example from my life:

I rise from bed in the morning, sit in a chair, clasp my hands above my head, and shake them. This is part Qigong, helpful for my asthma, nasal congestion, and energy. I have never been taught this exercise, but the body has me doing it. And for me, it works.

The body's intelligence directed this movement, not thought or planning. I have a background in kung fu, Qigong, yoga, etc., yet the body directed these different automatic movements out of intelligence to correct issues with physical structure and internal health.

After the exercise, I sit down to write. Thought might come in at some point and say, *Good day for a walk.* Also, thought might say, *Good day to write eight hours and get a lot done.*

But the body might interrupt my writing, with my arm reaching for the phone. I stop writing, call a friend, and calmly pace my apartment during the call. I don't feel any concern about not writing now because I know that the body, intelligence, and mind are directing all of my action. And it will always be for the best HERE. I never went out for a walk that day and only wrote about four hours. But there wasn't conflict inside over any of it.

This process allows freedom from thought; from following thoughts, chasing them, or feeling you have to carry them out into action. Intelligence, mind, and awareness operate the body.

As you end rote illusions, intelligence blossoms.

REAL-WORLD STRESSFUL PROBLEMS

*How do we cope with things over which
we have little control?*

There are many world issues that people respond to with Self-Created Stress. Climate change. Plastic pollution. Toxic chemicals. Rising human and domestic animal populations. GMOs (genetically modified foods and animals). War. Political fighting. Crime. Ocean acidification. Racism. Whales and coral reefs dying. Poverty. Starvation. Gun violence. Immigration. Violence against women. The slave trade. And more.

Unfortunately these are all real-world problems.

With our busy lives, it may seem easier to ignore the larger issues plaguing the world. But what if we can't ignore them? People living on coastlines or islands are unable to ignore global warming as the oceans rise. And all of us are breathing in, eating, or drinking microscopic plastic pollution; even the fish we eat are consuming plastic!

What can we do besides bury our heads in the sand and ignore these problems?

If you see a real tiger, you run! You take action!

Let's examine one problem; global environmental issues, which includes many of the issues listed above. Within that larger issue, one massive problem is plastic pollution on land and in the oceans. Plastic is creating a toxic nightmare worldwide.

The plastic pollution problem might be with us for years or decades, and there is a tendency to react with Self-Created Stress and create an underlying, constant anxiety.

We can limit plastic use in our lives by avoiding shrink-wrapped items, plastic straws, plastic cups, plastic water bottles, coffee in plastic cups, etc., and make choices HERE that matter. We can vote for politicians who want to end single-use plastics, sign email petitions, and get involved in public awareness campaigns.

The real-world danger of plastic pollution may push you to be an environmentalist, or to become involved. Direct action helps us because we are taking action, not simply thinking and worrying. Take control.

I wrote a nationally endorsed book on environmental issues in 1994, and care deeply about the planet. I do what I can by buying organic food, avoiding toxics and GMOs, eliminating plastic from my life, avoiding plastic in products, and educating people.

I have participated in many environmental actions and groups. Alone, I cannot change governments or control large corporations. But I can vote for candidates who also want to respond to these problems and who also keep abreast of the many solutions.

What if despite taking action you are still stressed by these problems? Consider these points:

○ Stress and worry won't help the outcome.

○ We can take these issues seriously without adding in Self-Created Stress.

○ We can act in every way possible, and let the rest go. If you're not satisfied with these actions, then do more. Act HERE. Don't dwell on the problem.

If you end your Self-Created Stress patterns, you will step outside of the rote neural patterns driving our world's problems. You will be living out of happiness and creativity. In that space, you may find a solution to help the whole world.

What else can we do?

Don't hold it in! Talk to other concerned people, such as an environmental group. You will feel connected instead of isolated, when you learn that others share your concerns and are working on solutions.

Continue body scans & deep breathing (Chapter 5), and continue to wake up your brain by ending Self-Created Stress patterns and illusions.

Environmental issues threaten our physical safety on the planet. Scientists have warned that the entire ecosystem of our planet is at risk of imminent collapse unless we make major changes. This is not a Self-Created Stress distortion or illusion we created, but a real tiger that is running at us full speed.

~

Why Are Humans Creating All These Problems?

Why have people created problems in almost every area of life?

Our societies are constructed by our thoughts, i.e., by the neural patterns we create in our brains. Men created capitalism based on *endpoint* ideas: future success, profit, power over others, acquisition of wealth and goods over time, etc. If we blindly follow our illusion-creating thoughts, decision-making and science are also held hostage to those same illusions of *endpoint* and *profit/material acquisition*.

Currently, the application of scientific decisions is often not based on intelligence, harmony, and love operating HERE. For example, current technologies used in corporate commercial farming practices poison the air, water, food, and our future. The same can be said about fossil fuels, plastics, toxic chemicals, cutting down rainforests, etc. None of this can be called sane, intelligent, or love by any standard.

If everyone woke up one morning and saw that our beautiful planet is in trouble, we would immediately change everything causing the problems. We would immediately revamp our society.

Again (from Einstein): "*Insanity is doing the same thing over and over again and expecting different results,*" and "*No problem can be solved from the same level of consciousness that created it.*"

Change yourself, your brain, your awareness, and you will change the world.

TRY THIS

Without trivializing world problems, the goal is to recognize them, talk about them, and live with them without adding more Self-Created Stress. Playful exaggerations can help us end our rote reactive stress patterns and give us the strength we need to face problems with sanity, and without constant anxiety.

Example:

If you have the underlying thoughts, *I'm worried that the oceans are going to die in the next decade. Then we'll have a food crisis and lose the beauty of fish, whales, and all ocean life!*

For a playful exaggeration you could say, *I am voting for the next alien arrival to be world ruler and clean up our planet!*

Or you could say, *I can't wait for the turtles and elephants to rule humanity!*

Interrupt any patterns of worried thoughts, replace them with playful exaggerations, and look yourself in the mirror and say, *I love the planet and will do everything I can to help all life here.*

Currently, solutions to the real-world problems facing our planet are decided by corporations that fund political election campaigns. Corporations act as feudal lords, and politicians mostly do their bidding.

Vote for politicians who want to save natural resources. Vote for the future home of our children to remain healthy and vibrant. Vote for term limits and an end to corporate funding of election campaigns.

Corporations only exist because consumers buy their products, services, or stocks. You have more power than you realize if you exercise your choices and avoid products of corporations that are damaging the planet and refuse to change. Don't add to their profits. Be vocal.

Real-world problems are dangerous tigers, and change is necessary. Waiting for the tiger to knock us down, or hoping it goes away, gives us a sense of futility, hopelessness, and stress.

Act.

PART 3
POWER EXERCISES

CHAPTER 13

Drama-Free Living with Names & Pronouns (Power Exercises #1 & #2)

All the people in your mind are YOU.

The four major types of illusions that people create are:

1) Internal conversations with "other people" (imaginary conversations)
2) Identification with the pronouns *I* and *Me*
3) Psychological time
4) Psychological location

In reality, all four of these illusions are usually taking place simultaneously in our thought process. However they are easier to understand if we examine them one at a time.

~

ILLUSION #1

Internal conversations with "other people" (imaginary conversations)

~

You are alone in your mind.

The use of pronouns and names in our thought process is one way in which the brain tries to organize our relationships with other people. Yet this process creates conflict, misery, and illusions.

Example:

Just before you leave your job for the day, a coworker tells you that you didn't do your assigned task. The worker is unaware that your supervisor asked you to do something else instead. You don't have a chance to respond. You go home with their comment in your head.

The Self-Created Stress dialogue inside your mind might be:

How can s/he say that to ME? The nerve!
It's really terrible. The jerk!

You support your Self-Created Stress reaction by repeating these reactions to others as gossip. Or you imagine yourself in an argument with the co-worker, yelling at them or defending yourself.

This thought process is not uncommon. It happens quickly in the brain, and isn't always easy to recognize. If you find yourself in an argument inside your mind, often those elements are all there in some form.

So what is happening?

In an inner argument or conversation, your thoughts are playing the role of you *and* the other person—but they are all *your* thoughts. You are, in effect, arguing with yourself, even though it feels as if you're arguing with the other person.

Accepting or believing that the thoughts and images in your mind are or represent the other person is an illusion. You can't have an argument with a *real* person in your mind or brain. You are not seeing them, hearing them, or talking to them.

When you have conversations in your head, you're telling the brain, *I am seeing this person, they are speaking, and I am speaking.* Yet the person isn't HERE.

You have created a contradiction to HERE, contradicting what your eyes and ears see or hear. You are overriding your optical and auditory nerves with imaginary images and words.

Thus there is a difference between what the senses observe HERE, and what your thoughts are telling you that you are 'seeing, hearing, and doing.'

That contradiction is illusion and stress.

Pronouns (*he, she, them, him, her,* etc.) in our thoughts/ brain are not another person. Nor are names such as *John, Mary, Bill, Sue.* Names and pronouns are not the total person, nor their body, mind, spirit, heart, the totality of their lives, or their personality.

Can you ever win an argument or convince an image or word in your brain of anything?

All the images in your brain are YOU! And images are not alive, not able to talk, and not whole people. They are just memory fragments. They are not the essence, spirit, or life of anyone.

The brain creates images for security, safety, love, and acceptance. Yet how can any image make us safe or loved?

The pronouns *he, she, them, they, us,* and *you* are frequently used in Self-Created Stress. For example, *How dare HE cut me off! How could SHE say that? THEY are all stupid. I hate THEM. They're not like US.*

If you hang on to these reactions, you will react to the pronoun the next time you meet the actual person or people.

Using the names of people (e.g., *John, Mary, Bill, Sue*) can have the same effect. Perhaps you think, *Sue was such a jerk to me!* Then, next time you see Sue, you might only be seeing that fragment of thought (*Sue was such a jerk to me!*), and not the actual *Sue*. The resentment and memory that you have about Sue becomes a filter between your eyes and you only see a small part of her.

Sue might have changed since your last encounter or want to apologize. Or not.

That doesn't mean you take abuse, but you also don't want to follow rote reactions in your brain and allow them to dictate your relationships with people. Those rote reactions (out of old neural pathways) create illusions, conflict, and the stress we are working to end.

Quickly venting to a friend, spouse, or coworker to release frustration can be healthy. Talking to others can give you perspective, understanding, or help resolve conflicts. But complaining, running someone down, and continuing Self-Created Stress is wasted energy.

~

How Do You End Imaginary Conversations?

Observe and watch the melodrama in your mind. Remind yourself that these names or pronouns are not the actual person, and the action isn't actually occurring or observable HERE. Then use playful exaggeration.

For "Sue," the woman who treated you poorly *(Sue was such a jerk to me!)*, you could say/think: *Sue treated me so poorly that I'll have to get a brain transplant!*

Exaggeration and humor will help you put events into proper perspective, interrupt the pattern, change it, and allow you to escape your rote reaction. Your brain is always listening to your intent. Is your intent to be right? To get back at Sue or punish her? Or to change your conditioned brain?

Everyone wants to be loved, to love, and to be happy. Some of us have easier roads to travel than others, with more help along the way. Some of us are more gifted than others, through genetics or environment, in finding harmony. Recognize this, and it will build empathy inside you for anyone who is acting out of their own Self-Created Stress. And you will be less likely to react to them with your Self-Created Stress.

See through your labels to the person in front of you, and try to find a way to reach their heart instead of reacting to their conditioned Self-Created Stress responses.

~

Note: You might think, *Well, sometimes the imaginary conversations in my head feel calm and nice. Why should I bother ending them?* **All illusions divide our awareness and attention, and thus create conflict and stress.** Have the conversation with your friend or loved one in person or on the phone. Otherwise you might find yourself running a red light in your car while "talking" inside your head.

TRY THIS

1) **Power Exercise #1: This exercise is a powerful— and easy—way to end illusionary conversations.**

   Let's say you begin an imaginary conversation with John. Interrupt it as soon as you become aware of what you are doing, and say out loud, *There's Peter! Mary! Jack! Bill! Superman! Bugs Bunny!* etc.

Use names of people in your life and add in some fantasy, silly, or playful names too. As you say the names, visualize the person or character's face or name briefly. Look around you, as if the people and characters you name are standing far away, close, or in different directions.

When performing this exercise, don't respond to any of the names with further thoughts. If you do, bring yourself back to the task and try it again.

Smile when you do this! If you're not alone, thinking these statements works too. Usually a combination is best.

PAUSE HERE TO PRACTICE POWER EXERCISE #1; INTERRUPT INTERNAL CONVERSATIONS BY IMAGINING BOTH REAL AND FICTITIOUS PEOPLE AROUND YOU WHILE SAYING OR THINKING, *THERE'S FRANK, THERE'S BATMAN, ETC.*

Power Exercise #1 trains the brain to not react to a thought (a person's name or image) as the actual person. It stops the brain from adding more thoughts to the imaginary conversation. By adding fantasy characters (Peter Pan, Captain Marvel, Spiderman, etc.), it helps strengthen your brain and mind's ability to see the illusionary quality of what the brain is doing when it creates a conversation with an image.

Imaginary conversations begin to fade away. The brain begins to see them for what they are—just thoughts—and the neural net that is creating them begins to fade away. This results in focusing on HERE with increased awareness and joy.

What Will Happen To My Relationships If I Don't Think About Them?

An image of someone is NOT the person. Images are old, incomplete memories. Relationship is HERE, based on interacting with the person HERE, not an illusion. This doesn't mean you lose love for someone or forget them. But it does mean that you relate to them HERE.

People sometimes feel their partner has changed and doesn't match their memories of them. Life is change, for all of us, at any age. The constant in relationships is love, accepting change, and not trying to trap someone into matching your memory of them. The brain constantly tries to find security in all relationships, but there is no security in relating to images instead of the real person HERE.

Often images in our brains are replayed repeatedly as we drag the same images from HERE to HERE to HERE. Dragging the same old, fragmented images to new places takes our "baggage" wherever we go.

It takes enormous energy and attention to constantly create the same repetitive images and fabricate conversations with those images/names in our brains. To give those conversations such importance requires you to override your senses HERE and contradict them with fragments of illusions.

Talking to an image or name in your brain will never feel complete, finished, or whole. That sense of incompleteness creates stress (inwardly and outwardly), unaware relationships, and accidents.

The brain wants to know (and plan) what it will say next time you meet a person, but you can't do it until you meet the person again (or get them on the phone). You will have to surrender to the unknown and be vulnerable to HERE.

After I began investing energy in Power Exercise #1, it took me about two weeks to feel/be aware of the brain shutting down imaginary conversations before they began. When you interrupt imaginary conversations, you become more aware of the thoughts in your brain. It is a noticeable, real shift in awareness of how your brain operates!

2)   Another slight variation on Power Exercise #1:

Let's say you find yourself perseverating on someone's name or image out of worry, fear, or anger.

Perhaps you imagine speaking to *John in his cubicle at work*. You imagine a fragment of his image or face, and his name. Substitute images and names of silly characters like Bugs Bunny or Superman, for John. Imagine you are saying the same words/thoughts to those silly images instead of to the image of *John*.

Since all images are the same, i.e. fragmented memories that cannot speak or interact, it will help to end the perseveration on *John's image and name,* and help the brain to end the illusion that you are speaking to *him* in your brain.

Speak to John in person. It that's impossible, then at least stop inflicting stress, pain, and illusion upon yourself.

3) If you find yourself in an argument in your mind, ask yourself these questions:

    Is this person really in my brain/mind?
    Can I really argue with this person in my brain/mind?

4) Find an empty room, stand at one end, and look across it. Argue out loud with the person/people you are creating a conflict with in your mind. Stamp your feet, gesture, and say silly things to them.

    By exposing the absurdity of the situation to yourself, you will build awareness of this illusionary pattern and eventually find it impossible to carry on arguments in your head. This will lower your stress and the amount of energy you put into any real-life conflicts or challenges you are faced with.

PAUSE HERE TO ARGUE OUT LOUD IN A SILLY WAY IN AN EMPTY ROOM WITH SOMEONE YOU ARE IN CONFLICT WITH.

5) If you find yourself arguing with someone in your mind, you can also say, *I'm not arguing with that word or image! I'm not arguing with that name! I'm not arguing with myself!*

    This is factual, because the name or image in your brain isn't the person, it's just YOU.

PAUSE HERE TO SELECT A RECENT INTERNAL ARGUMENT YOU'VE HAD AND TRY THE ABOVE STATEMENTS OF; *I'M NOT ARGUING WITH THAT WORD OR IMAGE, WITH THAT NAME, OR WITH MYSELF!*

6) A slightly different variation on #5:

    Let's say you're in an argument with the image or name of *Peter.* If your name is *Mary*, you can say or think, *Mary is arguing with Mary* while still imagining the image and/or name of *Peter.* You can continue this with anyone you talk to in your mind, e.g., *Mary is debating with Mary, Mary is upset with Mary, Mary is chatting with Mary*, etc.

    If you draw the image or name for *Peter* on paper, it wouldn't *look* like *Mary*. But the point is that the images you mind-talk with are all YOU. No one else is in there. By using your own name, you are informing your consciousness and brain that you no longer believe in the illusion of talking to Peter.

    This is important, simple, and complex. This exercise is a powerful way to wake up your mind to the illusions your brain creates in internal conversations. (**Note:** Saying *Mary is arguing with Mary* is better than saying ***I am arguing with Me***. This is explained later.)

7) Every time your brain creates the image of another person in your thoughts, interrupt as quickly as possible and say, *Hi _____* (insert your own name here). This reinforces to your consciousness and brain that all images are YOU.

8) When an image of someone else is regurgitated by your brain, ask yourself, *What do I need/want that image to say? What do I want that image to believe? To do? To give me? Do I need that image to give me permission? To validate me? To accept me? To listen to me? To make me feel safe or loved? To believe something?*

See which of these questions resonate. No image of another person in your brain can say or do any of this! So why give any image that kind of power over you?

By practicing any of these exercises, you break down illusions of imaginary conversations and instruct the brain that you don't want to follow them anymore. You are forcing the brain to be aware HERE. Play with this, have fun, persist, and smile!

~

ILLUSION #2

Identification with the pronouns *I* and *Me*

~

I & Me are not YOU!

Many powerful illusions that people create every day involve the pronouns *I* and **Me**.

Just as pronouns (*he, she, they, them,* etc.) and names are not the totality of other people in our lives, the pronouns *I* & **Me** are not the totality of YOU.

There is no other word in our thoughts that individuals identify with more strongly than *I*, and thus by default, **Me.**

People will die, go to war, start a fight (verbal or physical), cheat, lie, be selfish, and do almost anything to protect their *I* and *Me!*

Why?

At some point in our evolutionary process, the brain identified with the word *I* as the complete representation of ourselves, our body, and our survival. The word *I* became the centerpiece of our language and the focus of everything important in our lives. Ideas and speech that began with *I* triggered strong emotional reactions. If the *I* feels threatened, then the brain assumes, *Tigers are attacking us!* and that our survival is in jeopardy, even when this is not the case.

When the brain also uses *I* statements, it inflates self-importance and the importance of our thoughts. These thoughts create conflict, stress, division, danger through distraction, and limit awareness.

So, how important is the word *I*?

The words *I* and *Me* are not your body's 37+ trillion cells, and not your brain's 100 billion neurons. They are only words or thoughts that create the illusion they are YOU.

If we are not *I* or *Me*, what are we? We are very complex beings with bodies, energy, intelligence, and mind that hopefully operates HERE in whatever we are doing. We cannot possibly capture ourselves with a word/thought such as *I* or *Me*. Even 10,000 words cannot capture our complexity, let alone one or two.

Find out what you are, instead of limiting your perception with the idea and illusion that; *I and **Me** capture who I am. I should slavishly follow and defend the **I** or the **Me** when they are attacked!*

We often play out mind dramas such as, ***I need** my friends to listen to **ME!** **I have to have** that piece of clothing! **I want** a piece of cake now! **I must have** this!*

We believe the word *I* is our whole being (body, mind, brain), when it is really just a rote thought and word coming out of a rote neural net in our brain. If we attach *I* to a sentence, we often believe it is vital for our well-being and happiness.

We end up in conflict with ourselves or others because our desires and expectations won't allow us to go with the flow. Instead we're captive to *I need, I have to have, I want, I must have*—and these thoughts too often dominate our actions and responses.

When you hear yourself begin a sentence with **I need, I must have, I want, I believe**, stop and consider if this is really something important or essential, or from a rote habit. Determine if you are controlled by the *I* or **Me** in your brain.

I want are probably two of the most selfish words on the planet when we refuse to consider their impact. Another result of attachment to the *I*, is that people equate freedom with "being able to do as *I* please or choose." But in reality you are not free at all. Instead you're under the control of your brain's old neural programing.

True psychological freedom in life is ending the repetitive reaction to your brain's rote neural responses, thought patterns, and illusions.

YOU are not the *I* in your mind. If you end the identification with *I* or **Me** in your thoughts, your over-reactive ego and inflated self-importance will be replaced with a healthy life perspective.

TRY THIS

1) **Power Exercise #2: This exercise is a powerful— and easy—way to end identification with the *I* and *Me* in the brain as *YOU*.**

To weaken your intense identification with *I*, substitute different letters of the alphabet for it. If you find yourself thinking, *I think...I need...I have...I can't...I believe*, rephrase the sentence/thought *I think* with another letter. **A** *thinks...***B** *thinks...***C** *thinks...***Z** *thinks* ...etc. For an internal conversation with

I, (e.g., *I am talking to John.*) substitute, ***A*** *is talking to John…****B*** *is talking to John…*etc.

Substituting different letters will:

- ○ weaken your identification with the pronoun *I*,
- ○ help break up the illusion that YOU are actually talking to someone else in your brain.

Use as many letters of the alphabet as you like. Your intention is to playfully end the intense identification with *I* or ***Me*** as YOU. This will allow you to see and feel differently about the thoughts you were clinging to for perceived happiness, which are actually causing you stress and misery. You will be less defensive about protecting *I* and ***Me***, and reacting out of *I* and ***Me***.

You can also use this type of substitution for actual events. Let's say you are out walking; you can redo sentences such as, *I hear birds singing; I see a blue sky; my legs are relaxed*; with, *B hears birds singing…K sees a blue sky…W's legs are relaxed,* etc.

This is another way to inform the brain that *I* is not the totality of who you are, and that you no longer want to identify with it as YOU. It is a way to be objective about yourself and lessen identification with the *I*.

PAUSE HERE TO PRACTICE POWER EXERCISE #2, BY SUBSTITUTING DIFFERENT LETTERS OF THE ALPHABET FOR *I* IN THOUGHTS OR FACTUAL STATEMENTS.

2) You can also use other playful substitutions for *I* or ***Me***.
Example 1:

Anytime you begin a thought with *I*, interrupt it and replace the *I* with a series of names (fictional and silly). Thus, *I believe that politician is the best!* can become *Frank, Susie, Mark, Fred, Bugs Bunny, Superman, Goofball believes that politician is the best!*

By substituting other names (real and fictional) for the *I* pronoun, you weaken the identification with *I* in your thoughts. You are telling the brain you want to end repetitious illusions.

PAUSE HERE TO TRY THIS EXERCISE NOW BY SUBSTITUTING NAMES OF REAL OR FICTITIOUS PEOPLE FOR *I* STATEMENTS.

Example 2:

You think; *I hate traffic!* Interrupt that chain of thought by changing *I* to *Apple,* and repeat *Apple hate traffic!* or *Doughnut hate traffic!* If someone cuts you off in traffic, and you think, *How could they do that to ME?!* Substitute something equally as playful for the **ME**, such as, *How could they do that to the King/Queen of the Road?!* or *How could they do that to Froggie?!*

All of the above exercises will do three things:

1) Weaken your identification with the *I* and **Me** in your thoughts.

2) Make situations less personal and more objective.

3) Force the brain to end the rote neural patterns that make the *I* and **Me** pronouns feel so important in your life.

On your deathbed, thinking about what was important in your life, you won't care about someone cutting you off in traffic. Or believe that your identification with *I* or **Me** as **YOU** is all that you are.

Playful substitutions can be used for any *I* or **Me** thoughts or statements, even if they don't feel stressful, because identification with them creates illusions. Weakening and ending your rote identification to *I* and **Me** can change your whole life!

PAUSE HERE TO WRITE DOWN THREE EXAMPLES OF *I* STATEMENTS. THEN SUBSTITUTE A PLAYFUL WORD FOR THE *I* PRONOUN IN THE STATEMENT.

Example:

I hate traffic could become, *Apple hate traffic!*

A) I Statement:

_____

B)   Playful Substitutions for I:

_____

Say, think, & visualize the playful substitution, and smile!

A)   I Statement:

_____

B)   Playful Substitutions for I:

_____

Say, think, & visualize the playful substitution, and smile!

A)   I Statement:

_____

B)   Playful Substitutions for I:

_____

Say, think, & visualize the playful substitution, and smile!

~

PAUSE HERE TO WRITE DOWN THREE EXAMPLES OF **ME** STATEMENTS. THEN SUBSTITUTE A PLAYFUL WORD FOR THE PRONOUN **ME** IN THE STATEMENT.

Example:

How could they say/do that to ME! could become, *How could they say/do that to Froggie!*

A)   Me Statement:

_____

B)   Playful Substitution for Me:

_____

Say, think, & visualize the playful substitution, and smile!

A)   Me Statement:

_____

B)   Playful Substitution for Me:

_____

Say, think, & visualize the playful substitution, and smile!

A)   Me Statement:

_____

B)   Playful Substitution for Me:

_____

Say, think, & visualize the playful substitution, and smile!

~

USE FIVE DIFFERENT LETTERS OF THE ALPHABET TO DESCRIBE WHAT YOU ARE ACTUALLY DOING, WEARING, ETC.

Example:

If you are going for a walk in the park on a sunny day, you could replace *I* statements with different letters of the alphabet; *L is walking in the park. B sees the blue sky. W is wearing shorts today. K loves the wind on her face.* You can do this virtually anywhere you are or during whatever you are doing.

1) _____

2) _____

3) _____

4) _____

5) _____

Use any of the above exercises whenever you find yourself creating stressful (or any) *I* or *Me* thoughts. Do it often, and be persistent! You will find your reactions softening, your stress lessening, and your smile widening over the playfulness of your statements and the silliness of the Self-Created Stress that can turn a minor event into a mountain.

End the *I* and *Me* reactions that leave you feeling angry, frustrated, worried, or stressed. Embrace your inner child's sense of playfulness instead, while ending your identification to a pronoun in your brain. This leaves you free to discover the complex YOU that no pronoun can ever capture! Rewire your brain to end the silly importance of *I* and *Me* pronouns, and Self-Created Stress surrounding these pronouns.

~

Note 1: *I* **need,** *I* **have to have,** *I* **want** statements are also strongly tied to habits and addictions. This is another good reason to minimize our identification with them. Identification with these statements gives us the feeling that if we don't get an item, we will be missing or lacking something, which will then lessen our happiness and well-being. Nothing could be further from the truth. When you hear others expressing strong *I* statements, it will help your own journey in ending this illusion.

~

Note 2: Thoughts such as, *S/he doesn't like me! I miss her/him!* create and *are* pain, stress, and sadness. If you identify with the pronouns *I* and *Me*, or believe *she, he, her, him* are the real person, then you've created—and believe in—an illusion. Essentially you are saying, *This pronoun (S/he) doesn't like this pronoun!(Me)* or *This pronoun (I) misses that pronoun (her/him).* Look in the mirror and say to yourself, *I miss that person, but the image (or name) is not him/her, and I can't miss an image because the image is in my head!*

PRACTICE

1) When you begin a needy *I* statement (*I need, I have to have, I want, I must have*), interrupt it and play with exaggerations. Replace *I* with something absurd, such as *Elephant need, elephant have to have, elephant want, elephant must have...* Or the replacement could be *Pickle need* or *Bowling pin need* etc. End the identification with the *I* and *Me* to step back and be objective.

2) Sometimes you may find yourself in real conversations where you're feeling something strongly. Your voice strengthens and you can feel energy surging in your chest or throat as the words come out; *I know...!* or *I believe...!* or *I don't agree!* or *Not Me!*

   When you create any sentence where you feel a powerful identification with *I* or *Me*, say, write, or think the following:

   Protect the I! or *Protect the Me!* And perhaps visualize a group of mice, or something equally silly, raising a flag with *I* or *Me* printed on it, or protectively surrounding giant *I* or *Me* letters atop of a hill.

   Interrupt, break the chain of acceptance, playfully exaggerate, and smile! *YOU ARE NOT THE WORDS I OR ME!*

3) Volunteer. One way to end obsessing about yourself and others is to volunteer and provide a service for those in need. To see others who truly have huge limits and challenges in their lives brings a sense of humility to your life, and places the *I need, I have to have,* etc. thoughts in your head into proper perspective.

4) We can overstress our body in diet and exercise by following the *I* in our thoughts.

If you think, *I'm going to do fifty pushups,* or *I'm going to run ten miles,* or *I'm going to starve myself,* and follow these thoughts blindly, you may hurt yourself. To understand the difference between discipline and blindly following goals requires paying attention to your body.

Maybe you're fatigued, and during exercise the body sends signals of pain or discomfort, indirectly saying, *Not today/HERE, please stop!* And perhaps your body would prefer if you slowly reduce calories or cut out junk food vs. starving yourself.

You can't hear the body's signals if you blindly follow goals.

Likewise, thoughts of, *I'm too lazy to exercise* or *I don't want to exercise,* can just as blindly lead you to not exercising or following a healthy diet. *I want to eat a bag of chips* is a rote response to seeing junk food, and not the body's intelligence telling you what is good for it.

Interrupt your *I* statements, use playful exaggeration, and listen to your body. Your body will always tell you what's best for it HERE.

~

Tribalism

Note 3: Pronouns also keep alive the notion of **Us** versus **Them**. Long ago, individuals without a tribe would have more trouble hunting, have no help when injured, nor be able to defend themselves against an enemy tribe. This is also true with wildlife. Solitary lions are at a much greater risk of dying. Belonging to a pride (group) of lions is as essential for their survival as it was for people belonging to a tribe. Thus the brain identified strongly with the pronouns **Us** and **Them**.

Identification with these pronouns is often the underlying basis for conflict, war, anger, hate, racism, and aggression between countries, groups, political parties, races, etc. We actively seek out who is *for or against us*, reinforcing the brain's identification with *I, Me*, and our own *opinions*. *Us* versus *Them* does not come out of love or intelligence, or HERE, but is based on illusion.

Politicians and news media reinforce tribalism to keep conflicts alive for financial gain, political power, or corporate control.

The pronouns *Us* and *Them* no more captures the whole essence of individuals in a group than *I* or *Me* captures our own individual essence. When you find yourself using these pronouns in any conflict, interrupt your Self-Created Stress statements, create playful exaggerations, and inform the brain you no longer wish to view the world this way. You want these old neural patterns gone!

The phrase *One World, One Family*, has never been more true or necessary as it is today if we are going to solve the problems humanity has created. It embodies love and intelligence instead of isolation, fear, and tribalism.

~

Violence

Note 4: Beating, rape, murder, war, slavery, and other forms of violence are examples of extreme conflict and stress, and an utter lack of awareness, inner peace, happiness, and joy. This is true for the perpetrators and the victims.

The vast majority of violence on our planet is committed by men, often against women. Violent men are not living HERE, and are servants to illusions. Women frequently experience assault, control, domination, or threats from men. Indigenous women are at especially high risk of violence.

When women speak out against injustice or try to change male-dominated governments, they are often targeted, abused, or even murdered.

Violent men are unaware that they are controlled by their brain's neural programming. They have heavily identified with the pronouns *I* and **Me** and **Us** and **Them** in their neural nets. They also define their identification with "men should be dominant to women" as necessary to their survival, despite it being an illusion.

Men make up the bulk of current armies, usually begin wars, and often are in charge of decisions that put profit ahead of the interest of people and the natural world. They view nature as a privately owned resource to dominate, control, extract, and use for personal gain. None of these beliefs protect men, their families, or anyone else, since they often result in poisoning everyone's air, water, and food.

These men are not fulfilled or living lives of peace or joy, but are half-asleep, completely run by their brain's illusions—and caught up in tribalism.

When the images and ideas in someone's brain have more importance than the real world, insanity is the result. For example, a corporation might support cutting down a rainforest for profit (thereby jeopardizing the whole planet) if the owners are controlled by the *future* idea and images of profit. This is similar to playing poker at the kitchen table, and counting the money you have won, while the house is burning down around you—and you started the fire!

At one point in evolution, some of the above traits might have been a basis for survival. Now, following these patterns in the brain threatens everyone's survival.

To stop worldwide violence and save our planet, we need the harmonious model of sustainability, fairness, equity, and living HERE. We need to completely revamp how our brains operate so we can have inner peace and security, and to allow health, peace, and joy to flourish.

As Wendell Berry so aptly said, "We do not inherit the Earth from our ancestors, we borrow it from our children."

CHAPTER 14

Psychological Time & Location (Power Exercises #3 & #4)

Be the master of your brain instead of a servant to it.

ILLUSION #3

Psychological Time

~

You are only HERE.

Psychological time is another illusion people create with Self-Created Stress. Psychological time is often part of our daily stress, often creating the illusion of "movement" through time.

What's the difference between "psychological time" and "external time"?

External "time" is an actual record of movement. Our planet orbits the sun in 365 days and spins on its axis to make one full rotation every 24 hours, forming the basis for our yearly and daily calendar. This consistent movement of the planet is real and helpful for organizing our lives. Watches, phones, and computers track it, often via satellites. Calendars based on this actual movement let us know about upcoming appointments and events. And farmers track the seasons, weather, and temperatures for planting and growing our food.

However, when the brain creates psychological time, it steps out of reality and into illusion. We create illusions of past and future, which divide our attention and awareness from HERE. This is another example of Self-Created Stress.

We are partly rejecting HERE in favor of watching and participating in the illusion we create in the brain.

We think we move through the days of the week, months, and years, when actually our body moves from HERE to HERE to HERE, instead of through a time continuum in the brain.

I work in education, and when I have summers off, the days all blur together without specific names. Retired people experience the same thing where the day on the calendar is a word, not a FACT.

Monday is an example. Perhaps every *Monday* you react to going back to work or school with a habitual Self-Created Stress refrain, *I hate Mondays!* You lump all *Mondays* into the same dissatisfaction pile.

You have generalized a unique HERE with the label *Monday*.

You create the illusion you are moving through *Monday*, then *Tuesday,* etc., believing it is stressful, a downer, no fun. You believe *Monday* is real instead of being an arbitrary word that doesn't exist in reality.

Reacting to the word *Monday* makes it impossible to be fully present to any unique HERE. *Monday* creates negative feelings in you. This is a rote reaction and illusion responded to with a rote emotion. You have trapped your mind into believing that *Monday* is a FACT.

TRY THIS

1) **Power Exercise #3: This exercise is a powerful—and easy—way to end the illusion of psychological time in your brain.**

   Perform this exercise whenever your brain's neural net regurgitates a word denoting psychological time, future or past, whether or not it creates stress. This exercise involves other brain illusions and can change your neural conditioning.

If you are driving to work and think *Monday*, interrupt the thought and begin rattling off, *It's Friday, Wednesday, yesterday, ten years ago, 2050, Apple month, five seconds ago, Bouncing Ball Day,* or whatever you come up with.

Use playful terms to replace "time" words for "past" or "future". This reinforces the illusionary quality of psychological time and weakens the neural net that keeps this illusion alive. Don't forget to smile.

Intent is critical! Using playful exaggerations, you can make fun random word substitutions, while essentially telling your brain: *I want to live 100% fully HERE, without any time illusions of any kind! End this neural net process that creates the illusion of psychological time!*

The brain ALWAYS listens, even to your intent behind your thoughts and words.

PAUSE HERE TO PRACTICE POWER EXERCISE #3 BY SUBSTITUTING OUT LOUD DIFFERENT TIMES—PAST, PRESENT, AND FANTASY FOR TODAY'S DATE, TIME, DAY, YEAR, MONTH, AND SEASON. DO THIS EXERCISE EVERY TIME YOU HAVE A NEGATIVE REACTION TO A DAY OF THE WEEK, MONTH, SEASON, ETC. OR ANYTIME YOUR BRAIN GIVES YOU SOME THOUGHT OR WORD INDICATING TIME.

After beginning this exercise, it took my brain several months to lessen the creation of psychological time illusions. My old neural programming took that much time to substantially fade away.

The brain didn't default to creating time illusions because I wouldn't allow it. This strengthened the focus on HERE with increased awareness and peace. A few months of intermittent playful exercises that take less than a minute is a small price to pay to end a lifetime of conditioned responses and illusions. Eliminate the negative, and the positive will appear!

Although everyone is different, the brain requires repetition to rewire itself based on the feedback you give it. Be patient! You are fundamentally changing how the brain functions.

You may wonder, *What if I lose track of time?* Consult a calendar!

Whatever day you react to, *Monday, hump day, Friday, the weekend,* do Power Exercise #3 for it.

The name of a day is NOT the place/HERE. Society could have just as easily labeled the days *1* through *7*, or *Apples, Bananas, Carrots,* etc.

If you *hate January* because it's cold, play the same game. Say to yourself, *This is August, May, November,* instead of creating useless conflict and stress.

If you break down your old rote reactions and thought patterns, it will allow you to be fully HERE with your five senses.

~

FUTURE PSYCHOLOGICAL TIME

In college I often looked forward to weekend tennis, checking the weather and hoping for sunshine all week.

If it rained, I set myself up for major disappointment. If it was sunny, I was happy.

I wasted energy on the underlying conclusion and illusion of, *My peace of mind and happiness depends on playing tennis this weekend!*

It took me away from living HERE (which is a partial rejection of HERE), while I waited for a future time that only existed in my mind. The tennis appointment on the calendar was real, but the word *Saturday* in my mind was an illusion.

If you think/tell the brain, *I'm worried about Saturday!* it creates a contradiction. The brain is HERE, let's say in your house, yet you are telling it to be concerned about some image or word for a future day or time. The brain panics. It is HERE, safe and sound, yet you're telling it to be worried about some "future." That contradiction IS stress.

Other examples of this are:

○ *Waiting for winter to end.*

○ *Looking forward to the weekend.*

○ *Looking forward to an upcoming trip or event.*

In my twenties I planned sailing trips in the Caribbean. People asked, *Are you excited?* My answer was always, *Yes, but I'm just as excited about HERE too.*

I knew my life was HERE and refused to put my life or inner sense of fulfillment and happiness on hold until the trip. I refused to believe that; *I will be happier once I'm on the trip.*

We've been taught our inner peace and happiness are dependent on future events, that it varies and is not in our control. If we believe this, our psychological security becomes unpredictable, a prisoner to the whim of events, weather, or a change in seasons.

Excitement about an upcoming event is healthy, unless it diminishes or reduces peacefulness or awareness HERE, thus holding happiness hostage to the future event.

TRY THIS

1) If you find yourself dwelling on a "future" event, say to yourself:

Yes, this _____ (future event) *will be great and I will enjoy it! But I am not going to hold my inner peace of mind and happiness hostage to* _____.
I will be fully happy HERE. Fully aware HERE. Fully engaged HERE.

2) Playfully exaggerate the future event:
   - ○ *I will never be fully happy until* _____
     (day/event) *arrives!*

   - ○ *I am drowning in sorrow HERE!*

   - ○ *I am dead on my feet HERE! A walking zombie!*

   - ○ *This* _____ (future event) *will rescue me!*

   - ○ *I will have sparks shooting out of my head when*
     _____ (future event) *arrives!*

Or create something equally silly. Use a silly voice and words. Most importantly, have fun! Visualize your images as you think or say your playful exaggeration. And smile.

Create three playful exaggerations of a future event that you were or are looking forward to. Say, think, & visualize the playful exaggerations, and smile!

1) _____

2) _____

3) _____

PRACTICE

1) Another way to end the illusion of psychological time is through playful exaggerations that challenge the time illusion for upcoming events.

Example:

Let's say you're stressed about a dinner party on *Saturday.*

You may think, *I'm worried I won't be ready for the dinner party at my house on Saturday!* Which the brain might abbreviate to, *I'm worried about Saturday!* In a sense you are telling the brain, *A tiger is attacking me!*

Interrupt this illusion and play with it so you no longer react to the word/thought *Saturday* as if it is a dangerous FACT.

Create playful exaggerations such as:

I'm worried I won't be ready for the dinner party at my home on Monday! (or *Wednesday, Sunday, in July, December, May.*)

Deliberately picking a different date de-emphasizes *Saturday.* You are telling your brain not to pay attention to the negative neural patterns and to end Self-Created Stress responses caused by the illusion of a future time.

Playful substitutions inform the brain you refuse to accept *Saturday* as a FACT.

Look in the mirror and say, *"I have an upcoming dinner party. I will do all I can to prepare. It will be a blast!"*

Use **Power Exercise #3** every time an upcoming day or calendar date stresses you out. Eventually the neural pathway creating the repetitive rote response will fade away. Even without associated stress, we want to end the illusion of psychological time. All illusions create conflict and stress at some level.

This doesn't mean you shouldn't prepare for your event (wedding, party, date, etc.), but you shouldn't give any strength to the illusion creating stress around it. That stress won't make anything better, or make you more prepared.

2) Create three playful exaggerations for upcoming deadlines or events that you are worried or obsessing about. Use words for hours, days, months, years, or time in the past or future which don't match the current

calendar or your current watch/phone date or time for the event. Your intent is to change how the brain responds to upcoming events.

1)   A. Upcoming Deadline or Event:

_____

B. Playful Substitution Using Different Days, Times, Seasons, etc.:

_____

Say, think, & visualize the playful exaggeration, and smile!

2)   A. Upcoming Deadline or Event:

_____

B. Playful Substitution Using Different Days, Times, Seasons, etc.:

_____

Say, think, & visualize the playful exaggeration, and smile!

3)   A. Upcoming Deadline or Event:

_____

B. Playful Substitution Using Different Days, Times, Seasons, etc.:

_____

Say, think, & visualize the playful exaggeration, and smile!

~

PAST PSYCHOLOGICAL TIME

There is no past psychological time. Thoughts in our brain about the *past* give the illusion of a past; but memories are just thoughts. We might replay a thought about a verbal hurt from ten minutes, ten weeks, ten months, or ten years ago.

But the fact is we cannot replay actual events over in real life. And thinking about it may make us feel the hurt repeatedly in our mind, even without it happening HERE.

We can be safe and healthy, and yet recreate and feel psychological conflict or pain.

Example:

Let's say a week ago your friend John said something hurtful and painful to you. Your reaction is, *I can't believe John said that to me last week!*

Your thought is based on a past event. And yet you experience the thought and any associated images as if the pain of the event is occurring HERE. Thus you keep replaying the hurt or pain every time you think about or meet John.

Replace *I can't believe John said that to me last week!* with a playful exaggeration using substituted words and visualizations. *I can't believe John said that to me 500 years ago!* This will weaken the old neural pattern and give the brain other options. Remember to smile! Smiling is the emotional glue you want in your brain, not frowns and grimaces.

TRY THIS

1) Some thoughts feel like future thoughts, while others feel like past thoughts. Yet all thoughts are HERE in your brain. Thoughts can't be behind you or ahead of you even though they give the illusion of a past or future time. Whenever you have a thought of past or future, play with the thought.

Example:

Let's say you remember fragments of a conversation with your boss, such as, *Two years ago my boss was a jerk to me!* Replace *Two years ago* with *Ten days from now, two years from now, fifty years ago, five seconds ago, etc.*

You are breaking up this time illusion and exposing it to the brain. You are informing the brain of your INTENTION that you won't accept this type of illusion anymore.

~

Note 1: We discussed earlier that talking to images or names of others in our brain creates illusions. However these illusionary conversations also create the psychological illusion of time. Whether replaying a past conversation or imagining a future one, the fact is we are not talking to this person HERE. This contradiction to fact is worry and stress. The brain attempts to gain psychological security by analyzing the conversation or replaying it. Yet the brain cannot know what lies ahead, and cannot act on this conversation HERE. Thus your brain is frozen in inaction. You are creating an illusion and stress.

~

Note 2: Our society bombards us with messages that keep the illusion of psychological time alive. Ads talk about living for the weekend, a vacation, or the end of the week. Or saving up for some future purchase that will make us happy. TV shows and movies show characters doing the same thing. Why? The writers of ads, TV shows, movies, etc. are themselves lost in these illusions and don't even know it.

As your brain's neural net changes, you will begin to hear other people's rote psychological illusions as they talk. When you hear others doing this, it will further awaken your own understanding of how psychological time illusions keep all of us from living HERE with 100% clarity.

Note 3: Our society promotes desire, the anticipation of gaining something in the future. Marketing of products attempts to get you interested in purchasing an item, with the underlying promise that the item will make you happy in the *future*.

Desire is based on the illusion of psychological time, and is another version of expectations; waiting until you obtain something before you can be happy or fulfilled. Don't wait. Live HERE. Inner peace and happiness are HERE for the taking.

~

Note 4: The idea of living in the *present moment* or *the NOW* also contributes to the illusion of psychological time. If there is a *present moment*, or the *NOW*, there must also be past *moments* and *future moments*. This is subtle, but the brain will be aware of it, as will your mind.

Thus it is better to talk of living HERE. Clarity in how you talk to yourself matters in everything!

HERE is the only FACTUAL state of our existence. But HERE you can also be connected to the whole Universe.

~

ILLUSION #4

Psychological Location

~

Again, you are only HERE.

Psychological location in our thoughts is another illusion, and adds to the illusion of psychological time. You can't be in two places at the same time. Thus when you imagine, say, an image of a room in your home, your workplace, or a grocery store, those images are not the actual place. Yet we react to them as if they are HERE.

Example:

Perhaps you are thinking, *I have to get to the grocery store ASAP to get my shopping done!* You feel stressed. And you react to the image or word of *grocery store* as if it's the actual place, when it obviously is not. Just as the thought *I* and *Me* is not the totality of YOU, neither is the thought *grocery store* the totality of the actual store.

Look at this statement again; *I have to get to the grocery store ASAP to get my shopping done!*

First, it's impossible to "get" to an image in your brain. The image is in your neural net in your brain. You can't "get" any closer to it. Thought says, *I must **get** to the grocery store!* You are HERE, but want to be THERE; that contradiction creates an impossibility for the brain. The brain is being told it needs to be THERE, yet the brain is HERE, and it can't be in both locations at the same time. That contradiction is Self-Created Stress.

You are essentially telling the brain; YOU ARE NOT IN THE RIGHT PLACE! YOU ARE NOT WHERE I WANT YOU TO BE! YOU SHOULD BE AT THE GROCERY STORE!

The brain reacts with panic; *I have to be THERE, yet I'm HERE!* The brain immediately responds to this contradiction by tightening your stomach, hands clenching the steering wheel, and thoughts racing. You drive faster, adrenaline is pumped through your body, and you feel 'stress'.

The FACTS are most likely that you are safe, warm, and comfortable in your car. Your stress doesn't match the facts of HERE; it only matches the illusions in your brain.

If this is confusing, or only partially clear, we will get to clarity another way.

You can break up and reject the brain's Self-Created Stress illusion with playful exaggeration. Thus for, *I have to get to the grocery store ASAP to get my shopping done!* you can substitute something silly for *grocery store,* such as, *I have to get to the* **Leaning Tower of Pisa** ASAP *to get my shopping done!* Smile and briefly visualize what you can as you say this.

You can also substitute something playful for *ASAP*; *I have to get to the* **Leaning Tower of Pisa in five years** *to get my shopping done!*

Every time you feel stressed about having to get something done on time or be somewhere at a certain time, play with the illusion!

You might ask, *Well, how do I remember to get to the grocery store?* When you run low on food, you know food is at the store, and you go shopping when you have time.

Thought is invaluable when it gives us a reminder to do something, take action, remember to bring your laptop, or buy apples, etc. But repetitive stress results in worry that moves from one event to the next and the next, endlessly, until you die. Better to put aside this illusionary, repetitive process now, once and for all. And better to permanently change the brain so you can live with intelligence HERE.

TRY THIS

1) **Power Exercise #4: This exercise is a powerful—and easy—way to end the illusion of psychological location in your brain.**

   Whenever the brain says, *I have to get to the/I need to get to the /I'm going to the* _____, (fill in the blank), repeat a string of playful locations to reflect back to the brain the illusion it is creating. It doesn't have to be a stressful statement or situation to be an illusion, or to use this exercise.

For, *I have to get to the grocery store!* you can say/think, *I have to get to the Taj Mahal, the Amazon jungle, the top of a giant ice cream cone, the bottom of the Pacific Ocean,* etc.

Any substitutions will do, and a half-dozen is a good amount to aim for. Use real places that are beyond your possible reach HERE, and some fantasy locations so the brain sees the absurdity of creating psychological locations. Smile when you do this!

In time the brain will begin to end the creation of psychological location until the brain no longer creates these types of illusions except when it is useful information. What remains is focusing on HERE, with increased awareness and joy. Master vs. Servant.

PAUSE HERE TO PRACTICE POWER EXERCISE #4 BY SUBSTITUTING DIFFERENT EXOTIC AND FANTASY LOCATIONS FOR THREE LOCATION THOUGHTS.

PRACTICE

1)   A) Think of three past or upcoming deadlines you have at different locations.

     B) Create playful exaggerations by substituting a different day or month for the deadline. Also substitute a different location for where your deadline is taking place.

Example:

A)   Deadline worry: *I'm concerned about the report I have to deliver at work on Monday!*

B)   Playful Exaggeration: *I'm concerned about the report I have to deliver at the gum factory ten years from now!*

PAUSE HERE TO PLAY WITH THREE EXAGGERATIONS OF TIME AND LOCATION FOR UPCOMING DEADLINES OR EVENTS THAT YOU HAVE RESPONDED TO WITH SELF-CREATED STRESS.

A) Deadline Worry:

_____

B) Playful Exaggeration with Time & Location
   Substitutions:

_____

Say, think, & visualize the playful exaggeration, and smile!

A) Deadline Worry:

_____

B) Playful Exaggeration with Time & Location
   Substitutions:

_____

Say, think, & visualize the playful exaggeration, and smile!

A) Deadline Worry:

_____

B) Playful Exaggeration with Time & Location
   Substitutions:

_____

Say, think, & visualize the playful exaggeration, and smile!

~

Internal conversations, identification with *I* and **ME**, psychological time, and psychological location are the strongest illusions that we create. The brain is attempting to organize itself with respect to action, and with respect to its relationship to everything and everyone. This leads to stress, illusion, and divided awareness. Be patient. The brain will change. Hold onto that intention.

CHAPTER 15

Mind Chatter

Can we end it, and why should we?

Often we have mind chatter; non-essential, sometimes random thoughts running through our brain, related to what we're doing, observing, where we are going, or about the people in our life. They are fragments of memories, conversations, etc., that create more illusions in the brain.

These thoughts might feel comfortable, not seem to cause anxiety, and may seem normal.

Perhaps our brain sees an advertisement and responds with thoughts, or replays a conversation we had with a friend, or rambles about any number of possibilities. Thoughts can also create desire and make us eager to experience or repeat something we already enjoyed. This is the opposite of disappointment, but involves the same process of rote repetition with a different emotional response—excitement.

Everyone has their own tapes running.

Why should we care about mind chatter if it's not causing serious stress or conflict?

Anytime you are running an old or repetitive thought tape through your brain, you're not able to focus fully HERE. **Mind chatter separates your awareness and creates a division between what you are observing outwardly with your senses HERE, and what you are thinking. That division is stress and limits awareness.**

Research shows that the brain cannot be fully 100% focused on two actions at the same time. Multitasking is real, but getting caught up in our thoughts while driving divides the brain's awareness. Distraction is the #1 reason for car accidents.[17]

We have all heard someone say, *I just drove there and don't remember any of it.* The driver was lost in his thoughts. Lost is a good way to look at it.

Another example is when someone is talking to us, and instead of listening, we're thinking about what we want to say or something else not even related to the conversation. This is embarrassing when the person speaking to you asks—*What do you think?*—and you look at them with glazed eyes. You have to ask them to repeat what they just said, because you have no idea what it was. You weren't 'paying attention'.

In reality, your attention and awareness were divided between what your senses were taking in, and the attention you gave the thought chatter in your brain. Thought chatter keeps us half-there and half-paying attention. You're not fully aware HERE.

This chatter is again rote repetitive thought patterns running through our neural net in the brain. They serve no new purpose, and always divide and lessen attention and awareness.

If you're running thought chatter patterns nonstop, the brain is on autopilot, running old neural patterns, and you are allowing them to occupy your attention. You follow them without any attached awareness or response. Half-asleep. This is the brain running you.

The reason we want to end Self-Created Stress is to be fully aware, alive, happy, and free of conflict. If we end

ceaseless thought chatter, we allow the brain to quiet and wake up.

Another form of mind chatter is creating fantasies to make ourselves feel good. The famous short story, *The Secret Life of Walter Mitty* (James Thurber, 1939, & 2013 movie by Ben Stiller), is about a man who daydreams heroic adventures. Fantasies and daydreaming may make you feel good, but are illusions that can keep you stuck, create dangerous accidents, and put you asleep at the wheel, so to speak. Again, we are not talking about actively, creatively visualizing goals here.

Mind chatter strengthens the illusions of psychological time and psychological location. Mind chatter also often emphasizes *I* and *Me*. This chatter might make us feel safe and comfortable, but can also present a real danger.

So what can we do?

TRY THIS

1) Whenever you find yourself caught up in mind chatter, such as rambling about a past conversation, an upcoming event, or something you observe, create a playful exaggeration.

Why?

You interrupt the rote pattern and force the brain to do something else. The message to your brain is, *I no longer find this repetitive chatter useful and want it to end.* By not following the chatter and by introducing something playful, the brain must pay attention to the changes.

Example:

Let's say you just spent the evening with John, whom you love, and had a great time. He said some nice things, and while driving home you repeat his words to yourself over and over. You think of John and see images of him. Yet John isn't observed by your eyes. He isn't HERE in your car. And the images of him are distracting you from HERE. Those images are dividing your attention from driving.

You could say out loud, *John, I'm sorry, but you're not HERE now, so adios!* Or you could playfully say, *I see John in my rearview mirror, side mirror, or on the trunk of the car!*

You could also say to yourself, *Hey, I love you, John. I had a great time, and we'll talk soon. You are not HERE, so I won't spend time talking to a word or image in my brain. John, you are not a word or image!*

Sound silly? So is talking to words and images in your brain repeatedly, or risking an accident by entertaining illusions. Interrupt. Playfully exaggerate. Visualize if you can. Smile.

PAUSE HERE TO PRACTICE SAYING OUT LOUD PLAYFUL AND FACTUAL STATEMENTS OF SOMEONE YOU ARE REPEATEDLY 'TALKING TO' IN YOUR MIND.

2) When you find yourself in mind chatter, pay close attention to your face, shoulders, jaw, or anywhere else that you tend to hold stress. Sometimes chatter is actually stressful without our realizing it. But if you pay attention, you will feel or notice it in the body.

 A) Do a body scan (see Chapter 5) to see if there is some area of your body that is tense over the chatter in your brain.

 B) Ask yourself if you are worried about silence. Some people fear quiet, and thus keep talking or thinking to fill up the silence.

 If that is the case, create playful exaggerations, such as,

 ○ *Oh, no! My brain is quiet! No one is talking!*
 ○ *I'm not thinking! I will turn into a stone and vegetate!*
 ○ *I'm melting into non-existence!*

○ *Without my thoughts running, I am nothing! I don't exist!*

PAUSE HERE TO PRACTICE THESE STATEMENTS NOW IF SILENCE IS SOMETHING YOU AVOID OUT OF WORRY OR FEAR.

It's good to use anything playful that will help you see the Self-Created Stress involved and the underlying exaggerated worries, fears, or concerns.

You might ask, *Without all my mind chatter, who am I? What am I?* This is a mystery to be explored. But you know that chatter divides your attention and awareness, and continues illusions in the brain. It is a dead, old habit. It limits love and intelligence HERE.

A quiet brain allows awareness and intelligence to flower into something new. Alive. It is nothing to fear or be concerned about. It will allow more peace and happiness in your life than mindless chatter ever can.

End the negative, and the positive will appear. You will get answers.

~

Note: As stated in Chapter 6 (Intuition & Self-Created Stress), sometimes thoughts might erupt in your brain to answer questions or solve problems. This isn't mind chatter, but intelligence and mind talking to us. These thoughts are used by intuition to inform us of a direction, and are not a passive, repetitive regurgitation of events that have already occurred. This is not what we are trying to end when we talk about *Mind Chatter.*

CHAPTER 16

Power Questions

Change only happens HERE.

In Chapter 6 we discussed using questions for intuition, and focusing those questions on specifics for which the brain could find answers, such as, *Why do I react negatively to George when he asks me questions about my family?*

We've discussed the brain's major illusions of internal conversations, identification with *I* and *Me,* psychological time, and psychological location. Now let's apply that understanding to questions we can pose to our brain to make fundamental, massive change. The brain must keep working on our questions, just as it does when we ask, *What was the name of that restaurant?*

Power Questions are aimed at creating change HERE. Change is always HERE. Any insight, realization, or ending of illusions, however small or large, always happens HERE, wherever we are.

Thus, instead of the brain slowly changing the neural net when confronted with interruption and rejection by our playful exaggerations, we can pose questions to see if the brain can find a way to shut down all illusions at once. A quantum shortcut.

Ask the following Power Questions and just listen in silence to the brain. Don't try to answer the questions with thought or think them through. Instead, pose the question, listen for the answer, and then move on.

You should still do the playful exaggerations and Power Exercises, which also force the brain to change.

If you say, *It's impossible for the brain to end all illusions at once!* you are telling the brain it's impossible. The brain will then NOT look for such a solution. Always keep the door open for possibility so that the brain can at least look.

This is true for anything in life. Better to say, *Let's find out what's possible* or *Anything is possible*, instead of putting limits on your brain. Better to have one of the best computers on the planet working to find a solution than to take it offline or sideline it in a search for one. Also, closing doors in the brain closes doors to intelligence and mind, and we want all doors open for any possibility.

Power Question Examples

1) Is it possible for the mind and brain to end all illusions of psychological time?

2) Is it possible for the mind and brain to end all illusions of psychological location?

3) Is it possible for the mind and brain to end all belief that inner conversations are real?

4) Is it possible for the mind and brain to end all identification with the pronouns *I* and *Me*?

5) Is it possible for the mind and brain to end all belief that images of people in my brain are real people?

6) Is it possible to end all belief that images in the brain are different from me/from _____ (insert your name here)?

7) Is it possible for the brain to be quiet, without mind chatter?

The above questions are samples, but basically reinforce what we accomplish with playful exaggerations and the Power Exercises. We inform the brain that we reject the current neural programming and won't accept illusions anymore. We want to end the pattern of Self-Created Stress. It's fine to change the questions, or come up with your own. We are all different and need to hear different words at times to learn.

Ask these Power Questions intermittently, with urgency, and listen for the answer. Allow your brain to work on finding an answer. It will help with the results you gain from playful exaggerations and the Power Exercises.

PAUSE HERE TO ASK AND LISTEN TO SEVERAL OF THE POWER QUESTIONS LISTED ABOVE.

CHAPTER 17

More Play for Persistent Rote Neural Patterns

Along the Road of Awareness

This chapter integrates strategies and ideas from the whole book and blends them into a playful method to break up and change rote neural patterns. We will also look at some new, very simple techniques. If some of the exercises feel awkward, don't worry; stick to the previous ones. Trust your intuition!

First we will use the same playful exaggeration techniques discussed before, but with an even broader effect. Earlier chapters introduced these elements. Here we will draw all four major illusions of Self-Created Stress together in one place.

When you have Self-Created Stress, you are basically creating illusions of time, location, identification with pronouns, and conversations. Of course, there are other illusions of activity (imagining yourself doing something) and imagining objects. But with all these illusions, you are overriding the senses. Again, if you are visualizing a result you want, that supports a goal or your health, that is a creative process. But often the illusions we create are rote reactions and just contribute to stress.

Example 1:

Perhaps while driving you replay a reprimand that your supervisor gave you the day before. And in your mind you defend yourself or have a conversation with him.

You might ask, *What if I'm thinking about the previous discussion with my boss to resolve a problem? What's wrong with that?*

While having this conversation in your brain, you're not seeing your supervisor, not moving your lips, not talking, and not hearing your supervisor's voice. The illusion is much like a dream when we are sleeping. And it takes energy, is stressful, and produces the psychological time illusion of future (you will be talking to him shortly) and past (the reprimand occurred the previous day). It divides awareness. You are not fully HERE. If you're driving, it creates a real danger of having an accident due to distraction and divided awareness/attention.

Thoughts create incomplete events that we can imagine, but that we can't act on or resolve HERE. Action is put on hold until you reach your job and supervisor. That delay between your thoughts and action is stress.

The brain wants to resolve the conflict now by talking to your supervisor, but it cannot because your supervisor isn't HERE.

Example 2:

Perhaps you're nervous about an upcoming presentation you have to make (at a wedding, at work, etc.). No matter how often you worry about how it will go and imagine the audience reaction, or your performance, you can't act HERE. The brain wants to resolve this uncertainty, but the presentation is not HERE.

That "space" or "distance" between thought and action is worry, stress, fear, disappointment, anger, and sadness. Our thoughts and the inability to act HERE *actually is* worry, stress, fear, disappointment, anger, and sadness.

So is there a way to tackle all four main illusions at once? Let's build up to it.

Example 1:

In Chapter 13 we changed *I hate traffic* to the playful exaggeration, *Apple hate traffic*. Let's also substitute the word *Horsies* for the thing we are upset about, which is—*traffic*.

> *I hate traffic* becomes, *Apple (I) hate Horsies (traffic)!* or
> *Doughnut (I) hate Mousies (traffic)!*

Just as the words *I* or *Me* are not YOU, the word *traffic* isn't the hundreds of cars with drivers rolling across the asphalt. The word *traffic* is a fragmented representation for what you are viewing, just as the words *I* or *Me* are a fragmented representation for you (your body, mind, brain, etc.).

If making two substitutions, such as *Apple hate Horsies*, feels too complex, then keep it simple.

For another example, if you are thinking, *How dare that customer/clerk be so rude to Me!* you could substitute *Froggie* for *that customer/clerk* so we now have:

> *How dare Froggie be so rude to Me!*

And if you want to take it further, substitute **Golf Ball** for **Me**, so we have

> *How dare Froggie be so rude to Golf Ball!*

Visualize the components of this sentence and smile!

Example 2:

Let's say your supervisor, Ben, is often crabby, and you react to him with daily Self-Created Stress. As you drive to work, you think, *I can't stand my idiot supervisor, Ben!* And you imagine him doing or saying something he's said before to you. Maybe you even argue with him in your mind. This can all happen in quick, rote fragments.

If you have a thirty-minute ride to work, in a subtle way you are assuming that in a half-hour (*time* illusion) you will have to deal with Ben's comments and behavior at work (*location* illusion).

Try a playful exaggeration with substitutions for time, location, your supervisor, and yourself. Thus, *I can't stand talking to my idiot supervisor, Ben, in a half-hour at my work building,* could become:

+ Name replacement:

I can't stand talking to my idiot supervisor, **Big Green Turtle,** *in a half-hour at my work building.* (replaced **Ben** with **Big Green Turtle**)

+ Location replacement:

I can't stand talking to my idiot supervisor, **Big Green Turtle**, *in a half-hour in* **the little mud swamp**. (replaced **my work building** with **the little mud swamp**)

+ Time replacement:

I can't stand talking to my idiot supervisor, **Big Green Turtle**, *in* **five years** *in* **the little mud swamp**. (replaced **a half-hour** with **five years**)

+ I/You replacement:

Big Corn Dog *can't stand talking to my idiot supervisor,* **Big Green Turtle,** *in* **five years** *in* **the little mud swamp**. (replaced **I** with **Big Corn Dog**)

You don't need to replace all the elements of a particular Self-Created Stress thought to succeed with your intention to end the rote illusion. These examples are presented to show how far you can take things to play with them, and to give you options of using any ONE of the substitutions in a playful exaggeration, so you're not limited.

In the above example, you could also add in a substitution for the activity you imagine yourself doing, which is *talking to*. Thus,

+ Activity replacement:

Big Corn Dog *can't stand* **dancing the tango with** *my idiot supervisor,* **Big Green Turtle***, in **five years** in **the little mud swamp.** (replaced **talking to** with **dancing the tango with)**.

Visualize yourself as a big corn dog doing the tango with a big green turtle in a mud swamp, and smile!

Feel free to make playful substitutions for any element in a rote neural thought that creates stress. One, two, or more substitutions for all the different elements is fine. Whatever feels easy, comfortable, and brings a smile to your lips, is right for you!

Your boss might still be crabby on a daily basis, but you will no longer be captive to reacting to his Self-Created Stress. You can smile, not take it personally, and perhaps get another job. You might even change your supervisor's Self-Created Stress reactions, even though the goal is to end yours.

As a note, changing the underlying thoughts/words of the *when* and *where* you are talking to Ben is important, because then you are rejecting the whole illusion. Ben could be dead, have an accident, be home sick, or be too busy to talk to you at all. Until you get to work, you have no idea if you will even see Ben. Or maybe you have a car breakdown and you never make it to work.

Life is unpredictable, and the brain uses thought to try to predict it. This unfortunately creates illusions that make us less aware and more insecure, and generates worry, anger, disappointment, sadness, and fear.

There are unlimited variations to dream up for the playful substitutions. You can use different variations on the same day, or on different trips to or from work. **There is no right or wrong or "best" choice of playful exaggeration substitutions. Whatever you choose is right, unless they are hurtful, angry, or sarcastic. You don't want to create more rote ill-tempered neural net reactions!**

Example 3:

For another example, let's return to Chapter 14, *I can't believe John said that to me!* And obviously John said it to you in the past—let's say *last week*—and he said it at a location—let's say a *restaurant*. The underlying thought is; *I can't believe John said that to me last week at the restaurant!*

Throw in substitutions for everything. A playful exaggeration of this is:

Chipmunk (I) can't believe **Bugs Bunny** (John) *took my acorns* (said that to me) **twenty years ago** (last week) **in the Sahara desert** (at the restaurant). Visualize it and smile!

~

To recap, what's important is that you:

1. Interrupt your Self-Created Stress illusions.

2. Weaken old neural patterns through playful exaggerations.

3. Say, think, & visualize the exaggerations.

4. Smile!

TRY THIS

1) Write down or consider difficult reactions you have to a person, situation, or event in your life. Then make one or multiple substitutions for the sentence that best captures your reactions. Lastly create a playful exaggeration with one or more substitutions.

Example:

A) Stressful Statement: *I'm so worried the package won't arrive here in time!*

B) Playful Exaggeration for: *I'm, here,* and *in time.*

   Little doll (I'm) is so worried the package won't arrive on Mars (here) five years from now (in time)!

A) Stressful Statement:

_____

B) Playful Exaggeration:

_____

Say, think, & visualize the playful exaggeration, and smile!

A) Stressful Statement:

_____

B) Playful Exaggeration:

_____

Say, think, & visualize the playful exaggeration, and smile!

A) Stressful Statement:

_____

B) Playful Exaggeration:

_____

Say, think, & visualize the playful exaggeration, and smile!

2) There doesn't have to be a 1-1 correspondence between your Self-Created Stress thoughts and your substitutions. Be childlike! *I hate slow rush-hour traffic!* could become *Horsies riding snails to the State Fair— giddyap!* or *Bears are stopping to eat at blueberry bushes.*

Remember to visualize the images in the exaggeration, and to smile.

~

MORE PLAYFUL EXAGGERATIONS

In this book there has been a progression of substitutions used in the playful exaggerations. We've also laid out a progression in understanding the illusions that your conditioned brain creates daily with psychological time, psychological location, labels, internal conversations, pronouns, and names.

But we can also simplify. When you first learned to walk, it was complicated, and involved learning how to balance, moving one foot ahead of the other, using your arms, and remaining upright on one foot at a time. After you learned to walk, it became simple. You didn't have to focus on all the separate elements; you just walked. It's no different with these playful exaggerations that we've used to challenge and end the brain's illusions.

TRY THIS

1) **Example:**

   You begin thinking about someone in a stressful way (arguing, trying to convince them of something, pleading, defending yourself, etc.). Perhaps a friend's facial image appears, possibly their name as well—*John*—and you think, *You're wrong, John!*

   You see where it's going and interrupt it.

You now know the illusions built into this kind of activity (psychological time, location, pronouns, and names), and thus cut off the Self-Created Stress thought, and create a playful exaggeration:

I see a flying horse over there! A hundred-foot-tall fire hydrant there! A giant orange rolling over the grass there! etc.

By doing this, you are replacing the name and image of your friend *John*, and the process of arguing with him, with obvious images that don't exist in your field of vision (what you are actually observing with your eyes HERE).

And while you say these playful exaggerations, glance at different locations where none of these objects exist. Don't forget to visualize what you can, and smile!

These fictitious objects (*flying horse, tall fire hydrant, rolling giant orange*) remind the brain that your friend John isn't here either. They break up the rote pattern and show the brain how silly it is. They inform the brain that you reject the initial illusion and also give the brain comparisons to other absurd illusions. All of this strengthens your awareness of the illusion you began to create in the argument in your head.

Consider a recent Self-Created Stress conversation in your mind with someone. Create three *I see a*_____ *over there!* playful exaggerations:

A) _____

B) _____

C) _____

2) Let's say in your mind you are arguing with John. You can interrupt the same Self-Created Stress conversation with *John* by saying, *I'm climbing Mount Everest, I'm swimming the English Channel, I'm riding a horse,* etc.

Again, these fictitious activities are no more real than the illusionary activity of you arguing with your friend, John. They interrupt the pattern, inform the brain that you reject the illusion, and strengthen your awareness of the illusion you began to create. Briefly visualize these activities and smile.

Consider a recent Self-Created Stress conversation in your mind with someone. Create three *I am*_____ (doing some absurd/untrue activity) statements.

A) _____

B) _____

C) _____

Everyone's conditioned patterns of thought and learning are different. Pay attention to your intuition, your gut sense of things, and use playful exaggeration techniques that work for you. In one situation, one playful substitution might be enough; in another, a complex exaggeration with multiple substitutions for time, location, labels, pronouns, and names might be better. What matters is INTENT.

Your mind will inform your intuition of what technique is best HERE.

It is still recommended that you focus most of your energy on the Power Exercises.

PRACTICE

1) There is another way to keep things simple. When you interrupt a Self-Created Stress thought, instead of saying or thinking of a playful exaggeration, just make a constant sound in your mind or speech to replace the brain's attempt to create those thoughts. The sound can be garbled, nonsensical, and used as a placeholder for thinking. This can rise and fall in pitch with your inhalations and exhalations.

This allows you to interrupt your usual pattern of thinking with one syllable, a few repeated syllables, or a string of syllables. Pay attention, smile, and have fun! The message to the brain is, *The old pattern of creating Self-Created Stress is no longer acceptable!*

You KNOW the goal is to end the creation of illusions in the neural net of your brain. You intend to rewire your brain. Without that intention, this becomes nonsense. The brain must listen. It will change. You're leaving it no choice.

This particular replacement is good for stopping mind chatter—the rambling of thought discussed in the last chapter.

PAUSE HERE TO CONSIDER THREE RECENT SELF-CREATED STRESS THOUGHTS, AND MAKE UP A SOUND IN YOUR MIND OR OUT LOUD TO REPLACE THE THINKING PROCESS.

A)   Self-Created Stress Thought to Replace with Sound:

_____

B)   Self-Created Stress Thought to Replace with Sound:

_____

C)   Self-Created Stress Thought to Replace with Sound:

_____

Make the sound for however long you want. Seconds or minutes are fine; no need for hours. Small bursts of repetition over time are useful.

It's okay to rotate from sounds, to simple playful exaggerations, to complex playful exaggerations, to Power Exercises.

Don't stop using playful exaggerations or the Power Exercises—words and images inform the brain in a way that garbled sound cannot. Sound is just another way to occasionally interrupt your Self-Created Stress. Trust yourself, and your intuition, to know what is best to use HERE.

2)   When you're upset with someone and are giving
      them a piece of your mind—literally, when you argue

with them internally—make up angry, garbled words. Imagine saying these words to a baseball bat, a donkey, or anything absurd. The idea again is to reject the rote neural pathways by interrupting them, replacing them with a playful exaggeration and substitution, and visualizing what you can. And smile.

PAUSE HERE AND THINK OF AN INTERNAL ARGUMENT YOU HAVE HAD WITH SOMEONE RECENTLY. CREATE GARBLED WORDS, AND SUBSTITUTE SOMETHING ABSURD FOR THE PERSON'S IMAGE.

Keep informing the brain of its illusions! And keep informing the brain of your intent to end them!

~

SETBACKS & GOALS

Anytime we try to change our body, brain, or life, we can experience setbacks, or a temporary plateau. Athletes, artists, writers, and anyone trying to push their limits experience this. If at times you feel that *Nothing is changing!* push through it. Try to be consistent with your response to the brain's illusions, and don't worry! Smile! Once you understand the illusions the brain is creating, you will have no choice but to keep going. You are the *Master!*

CHAPTER 18

A Quick Summary

Rereading this book is highly recommended!

1) Reread Chapter 1 definitions so you understand *Living with Intelligence HERE*.

2) Continue to use **playful exaggerations** as you work to change your reactions to daily events and your rote thought patterns. This will increase imagination and decrease mind chatter and all Self-Created Stress. (Chapters 4-12)

3) Always keep your intention in your mind. The exaggerations or substitutions are to end the mechanical patterned responses and to rewire your brain. Keep the process fun!

4) Review and apply the four **Power Exercises** to end the illusions of imaginary conversations, identification with *I* and *Me*, psychological time, and psychological location. Variations on the **Power Exercises** are fine! (Chapters 13, 14)

5) Begin using **Power Questions** to allow the brain to make quantum leaps in change. (Chapter 16)

6) Keep your brain healthy! Five essential things are exercise, minimizing screen time, sleep, time spent in nature, and a chemical-free diet (organic food if possible) that is rich in antioxidants (fresh fruit, veggies, and unprocessed foods). Whole foods are rich in antioxidants, and research points to this class of compounds (antioxidants) as essential to brain health. They are one of several areas implicated in preventing Alzheimer's and dementia. Get off screens as much as possible. Wear blue light blocking glasses.

7) Accept whatever life brings. This doesn't mean suffer or don't try to change it, but be at peace HERE, wherever that is. HERE is your world, is you, is your choice.

8) Listen to and trust your intuition! It will never fail you once you learn to trust it. (Chapter 6)

9) When you are caught up in Self-Created Stress, stop and ask yourself: *Is a tiger charging me right now? Is my life at risk? Am I safe, okay, HERE?* Exaggerate the situation. Play with it!

10) Look for beauty everywhere: in people, situations, and in nature. It's there if you look with an open mind, and it will make your life joy-*full*.

11) Find your passions in life, whatever your age, and pursue them. Try new things until you find what you love. Passionate people who love what they do for a job, hobby, or activity are generally happy people. They spend less time in negative reactions, and more time in calm, peace, joy, and love.

12) Visualize, and thus create, your dreams, goals, and even small events. (Chapter 8) Use visualization to assist your healing process. (Chapter 12)

13) If you had the best cheerleader or parent in the world, what would they say to support you? Say those words to yourself. Write them down, post them on the mirror, and read them daily. For example: *I'm a loving mother. I'm a caring friend. I do my best at school (or at work)— and my best is good enough.*

14) Whenever you find yourself on the verge of speaking negatively out of Self-Created Stress, find a positive and say it to yourself or someone else.

15) Breathe deeply, always, especially whenever you feel confused, discontented, or stressed. Inhale deeply into your stomach first, up through your torso and chest, and hold for 2-4 seconds. Exhale slowly. Focus on the air moving in and out past your mouth or nose. Don't strain during any of it. Repeat at least six times. Then do a quick body scan. (See Chapter 5)

16) Don't let pronouns rule your thoughts, your reactions, and your relationships. Be the master of *I, he, she, them, they, me, us, we,* and *you*, instead of the other way around. (Chapter 13)

17) Never stop reminding yourself of, and interrupting, your rote illusions. Illusions **are** fear, worry, anger, sadness, loneliness, and disappointment.

18) Remember, true psychological freedom in life is ending the slavish reaction to your brain's rote neural responses and thoughts. Keep that as your intent.

19) When you find yourself in Self-Created Stress that you can't immediately stop, don't beat yourself up. Exercise, leave the situation, and regroup. Relax, learn, and move on.

20) Change up your energy. Sing or dance, alone if you have to. Spontaneity is great. Switch up the old routines.

21) Laugh or yawn often. Laughs and yawns change brain chemistry for the better, are contagious, and can positively influence others.

22) Do you have personal photos of beauty on your walls, either of people you treasure or places in nature that you admire? If the answer is no, change your environment, because it will change you.

23) Tell yourself daily in the mirror, *I love you!* And after any task, *Great/Awesome job,* _____ (insert your name here)!

24) Smile daily. At everyone. It helps you, even if others don't smile back. Smiling takes years off your appearance and adds years to your joyful life. Smile at yourself every time you look in the mirror. A smile instantly places you into a meditative state.

Smiling has been positively correlated by research with success, longevity, health, and happiness. Smiling lowers your heart rate. British researchers found that one smile has the same positive level of stimulation for the brain as eating 2,000 chocolate bars![18]

Author's Note

Thank you so much for reading *SMILE MORE STRESS LESS*. I lived a large part of my life in constant anxiety and worry. I still use the playful methods in this book, and love the freedom they have given me from stress, and the resultant awakening of intelligence.

I loved writing this book, and hope you enjoyed reading it. More, I hope it helps you leave stress behind and allows you to smile more!

Reviews help me keep writing, and encourage other readers to take a chance on a new author they haven't read before. So if you enjoyed the book, and found it helpful, please leave a review! Every review, even a few words, helps!

Thank you!

~ Geoff

Bibliography

Sources Cited—All accessed October, 2020

1) Guntuku, S. C. et al. (2018). "Understanding and Measuring Psychological Stress using Social Media" *https://www.researchgate.net/publication/329030683_ Understanding_and_Measuring_Psychological_Stress_ using_Social_Media*

2) Welsh, T. (2015). "What is the speed of thought?" *https://earthsky.org/human-world/ what-is-the-speed-of-thought*

3) Hayakawa, S. et al. (2019). "How Language Shapes the Brain" *https://blogs.scientificamerican.com/observations/ how-language-shapes-the-brain/*

4) Hampton, D. (2017). "The 10 Fundamentals of Rewiring Your Brain" *https://www.huffpost.com/entry/ the-10-fundamentals-of-re_b_9625926*

   Olson, H. (2019). "Can I Rewire My Brain?" *https:// mcgovern.mit.edu/2019/09/06/can-i-rewire-my-brain/*

5) Griffin, R. M. WebMD. (2014). "10 Health Problems Related to Stress That You Can Fix" *https:// www.webmd.com/balance/stress-management/ features/10-fixable-stress-related-health-problems#1*

6) Sauer, A. (2017). "The 27 Stressful Life Events That Can Lead to Alzheimer's" *https://www.alzheimers.net/ the-stressful-life-events-that-can-lead-to-alzheimers/*

7) Arizona PBS. (2017). "Early childhood brain development has lifelong

impact" *https://azpbs.org/2017/11/
early-childhood-brain-development-lifelong-impact/*

8) Stevenson, S. (2012). "There's Magic in Your
   Smile" *https://www.psychologytoday.com/us/blog/
   cutting-edge-leadership/201206/there-s-magic-in-your-smile*

9) Weidman, C. (2017). "How Stress Can Change Your
   DNA" *http://sitn.hms.harvard.edu/flash/2017/stress-
   induced-dna-modification-may-play-role-mental-illness/*

   Marchant, J. (2017). "Language patterns reveal body's
   hidden response to stress" *https://www.nature.com/
   news/language-patterns-reveal-body-s-hidden-response-to-
   stress-1.22964* &

   Titlow, J. P. (2014). "It's Not Just For Your Brain:
   Meditating Can Actually Change Your DNA" *https://
   www.fastcompany.com/3040039/its-not-just-for-your-
   brain-meditating-can-actually-change-your-dna*

10) MCTFR, Minnesota Center for Twin and Family
    Research (2020). "Is Happiness Hiding in our Genes?"
    https://mctfr.psych.umn.edu/research/happiness.html

11) Horn, S. (2013). "Singing Changes Your Brain" *https://
    ideas.time.com/2013/08/16/singing-changes-your-brain/*

12) Kataria, M., MD. Laughter Yoga International. *https://
    laughteryoga.org/*

13) Li, D. (2014). "What's the Science Behind a Smile?"
    *https://www.britishcouncil.org/voices-magazine/
    famelab-whats-science-behind-smile*

    Savitz, E. (2011). "The Untapped Power of Smiling"
    *https://www.forbes.com/sites/ericsavitz/2011/03/22/the-
    untapped-power-of-smiling/#4821adf87a67*

14) Fader, S. (2020). "How Mirror Neurons Help You Relate
    to Others" *https://www.betterhelp.com/advice/behavior/
    how-mirror-neurons-help-you-relate-to-others/*

15) Morris, J. (2020). "The Protective Power of Purple Berries and How They Can Improve Brain Health" *https://www.bluezones.com/2020/04/memory-fruits-the-protective-power-of-purple-berries/*

Christiansen, S. (2018). "Alzheimer's Prevention Tools" *https://www.alzheimers.net/alzheimers-prevention-tools/*

16) Cordova, M. G., Cornell University (2020). "Spending Time in Nature Reduces Stress" *https://www.sciencedaily.com/releases/2020/02/200225164210.htm*

Cohen, D., Child Mind Institute. "Why Kids Need to Spend Time in Nature" *https://childmind.org/article/why-kids-need-to-spend-time-in-nature/*

17) King, E. L. (2017) "Top 15 Causes of Car Accidents and How You Can Prevent Them" *https://www.huffpost.com/entry/top-15-causes-of-car-accidents_b_11722196*

18) Gutman, R. Ted2011, "The Hidden Power of Smiling" *https://www.ted.com/talks/ron_gutman_the_hidden_power_of_smiling?language=en#t-78481*

Acknowledgments

This book would not be as wonderful as it is without the help of a number of people. Lauren Lein critiqued a very early draft. My lifelong friend and sailing/swimming buddy Mark Olien provided several in-depth critiques that added clarity to the text early on, and helped prioritize what was important. Dr. Joseph E. McEllistrem, Ph.D. added insightful comments on the psychological aspects of the brain, and some editorial feedback.

My friend, cousin, and writing buddy, Steve McEllistrem, helped with edits on an early draft. My friend Dennis Grubich, MSSW, LICSW also gave me invaluable feedback on early drafts. Theresa Vaske helped with an edit and gave insightful feedback on a later draft. My sister Kathy also helped with feedback on a later draft. And my wonderful, loving parents as always supported my writing. Beth Birnbaum tightened the text and cut fluff of a later draft. Michael S., Kathy, and Mark O. all gave feedback on the final draft. Ken E. helped clarify an important point. Anna provided last minute structural edits and line editing. I am very lucky to have such inspiring people in my life, who have added to this book and made my life richer.

About the Author

Geoffrey Saign began his inward journey by practicing mindfulness at the age of fifteen. For fifty years he studied many modalities for mind-body calming and awareness, including Qigong, tai chi, kung fu, meditation, biofeedback, positive psychology, and many others. He co-designed and taught a cutting-edge, research-based self-awareness class to young adults for ten years. In 2020 the author experienced a major breakthrough in mind-brain-body awareness, which led him to *living with intelligence HERE,* and the resulting book, *Smile More Stress Less.*

He hopes this book will help readers of all ages reduce their own stress. Geoff loves hearing from readers, and you can contact him at *http://www.geoffreysaign.net*

Made in the USA
Columbia, SC
18 December 2021

52051379R00129